STUDENT UNIT GUIDE

NEW EDITION

CCEA AS Biology Unit 1
Molecules and Cells

John Campton

PHILIP ALLAN

Philip Allan, an imprint of Hodder Education, an Hachette UK company, Market Place, Deddington, Oxfordshire OX15 0SE

Orders
Bookpoint Ltd, 130 Milton Park, Abingdon, Oxfordshire, OX14 4SB
tel: 01235 827827
fax: 01235 400401
e-mail: education@bookpoint.co.uk
Lines are open 9.00 a.m.–5.00 p.m., Monday to Saturday, with a 24-hour message answering service.
You can also order through the Philip Allan Updates website: www.philipallan.co.uk

ISBN 978-1-4441-7864-7

First printed 2012
Impression number 5 4 3
Year 2017 2016 2015 2014

Cover photo: Fotolia

Typeset by Integra Software Services Pvt. Ltd., Pondicherry, India

Printed in Dubai

Hachette UK's policy is to use papers that are natural, renewable and recyclable products and made from wood grown in sustainable forests. The logging and manufacturing processes are expected to conform to the environmental regulations of the country of origin.

Contents

Content Guidance

Questions & Answers

Getting the most from this book

Questions & Answers

Exam-style questions

Examiner comments on the questions

Tips on what you need to do to gain full marks, indicated by the icon ⓔ.

Sample student answers

Practise the questions, then look at the student answers that follow each set of questions.

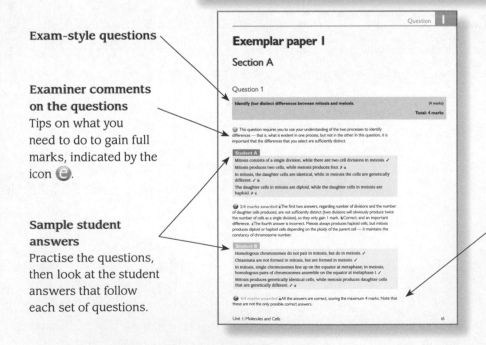

Examiner commentary on sample student answers

Find out how many marks each answer would be awarded in the exam and then read the examiner comments (preceded by the icon ⓔ) following each student answer. Annotations that link back to points made in the student answers show exactly how and where marks are gained or lost.

About this book

The aim of this book is to help you prepare for the AS Unit 1 examination for CCEA Biology. It also offers support to students studying A2 biology, since topics at A2 rely on an understanding of AS material.

The **Content Guidance** section contains everything that you should learn to cover the specification content of AS Unit 1. It should be used as a study aid as you meet each topic, for end-of-topic tests, and during your final revision. There are seven topics and for each there are *examiner tips* and *knowledge checks* in the margins. Answers are provided towards the end of the book. At the end of each topic there is a list of the practical work with which you are expected to be familiar. This is followed by a comprehensive, yet succinct, summary of the points covered in each topic.

The **Questions and Answers** section provides two exemplar papers for you to try. There are answers written by two students with examiner comments on the students' performances and how they might have been improved. These will be particularly useful during your final revision. There is a range of question styles, which you will encounter in the AS Unit 1 exam, and the students' answers and examiner comments will help with your examination technique.

Developing your understanding

It is important that through your AS course you develop effective study techniques.

- You must not simply read through the content of this book.
- Your understanding will be better if you are *active* in your learning. For example, you can take the information given in this book and present it in different ways:
  - a series of bullet points to summarise the key points
  - an annotated diagram to show structure and function, e.g. a diagram of a cell with labelled features and brief notes of function, or annotated graphs, e.g. showing enzyme properties with notes attached explaining the trends
  - a spider diagram, e.g. one on enzymes would include reference to theoretical aspects, the effects of temperature and pH, the effect of inhibitors and the effect of immobilisation
- Compile a glossary of terms for each topic. Key terms are shown in **bold** (with a few in the margin) and for each you should provide a definition. This will develop your understanding of the language used in biology and help you where *quality of written communication* is being assessed.
- Write essays on different topics. For example, an essay on enzymes will test your understanding of the entire topic and give you practice for the Section B question.
- *Think* about the information in this book so you are able to *apply* your understanding in unfamiliar situations. Ultimately you will need to be able to deal with questions that set the topic in a new context.
- Ensure that you are familiar with the practical skills expected in this unit so that you can answer questions on *How Science Works*.
- Use past questions and other exercises to develop all the skills that examiners must test.
- Use the topic summaries to check that you have covered all the material that you need to know and as a brief survey of each topic.

The AS Unit 1 paper

The AS Unit 1 examination lasts 1 hour 30 minutes and is worth 75 marks. There are two sections. In Section A all the questions are structured, though there is a variety of question styles. In Section B there is a single question, which may be presented in several parts, and which should be answered in continuous prose.

Be aware that the examiners must test a range of skills. These are called assessment objectives and are described in the CCEA biology specification. At AS, examiners must design the paper to show the following balance of marks.

Assessment Objective	Description	Marks
AO1	Knowledge and understanding	32
AO2	Application of knowledge and understanding	32
AO3	How Science Works	11

Questions towards the start of the paper and the initial parts of questions tend to assess straightforward knowledge and understanding (AO1). There will also be questions that present information in new contexts and may test your skills in analysing and evaluating data (AO2).

AO3 may be assessed by questions that ask you to evaluate experimental work. You may also be asked to demonstrate graphical or drawing skills, or to organise raw data into a table.

You are expected to use good English and accurate scientific terminology in all your answers. Quality of written communication is assessed throughout the paper and is specifically awarded a maximum of 2 marks in Section B.

Examiner tip
The CCEA biology specification is available from www.ccea.org.uk. You will also be able to access past papers and mark schemes.

Biological molecules

The chemical composition of living organisms

All living organisms are composed of atoms. The atoms occur as parts of small molecules (e.g. glyceraldehyde, $C_3H_6O_3$), large molecules (e.g. haemoglobin, $C_{3032}H_{4816}O_{872}N_{780}S_8Fe_4$), polyatomic ions (e.g. phosphate, PO_4^{3-}) and single ions (e.g. potassium ion, K^+). Only 20 different types of atom (of the 92 stable elements) occur in living organisms. The elements present in the largest proportions are carbon (C), hydrogen (H), nitrogen (N), oxygen (O), phosphorus (P) and sulfur (S). These atoms have low atomic mass and combine with one another to form molecules held together by strong **covalent bonds**. Consequently, living organisms are both light and strong. The remaining atoms occur as charged ions (e.g. Ca^{2+}, Na^+, K^+, Cl^-, Fe^{2+}).

The **water content** of living organisms ranges from 50% to 95%. Water is composed of hydrogen and oxygen; its formula is H_2O. Water is a liquid whereas other substances of similar molecular mass are gases (e.g. CH_4, NH_3, O_2 and CO_2). The reason for this is that water is a **dipolar** molecule (the oxygen is slightly negative, $\delta-$ and the hydrogen is slightly positive, $\delta+$), so neighbouring water molecules are linked by **hydrogen bonds** — weak bonds between the oxygen on one water molecule and a hydrogen on another (see Figure 1).

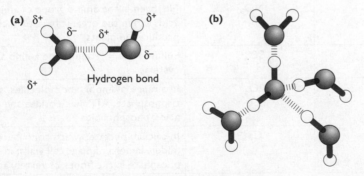

Figure 1 (a) The charges on water molecules; (b) a cluster of water molecules

Large carbohydrates such as starch, lipids, proteins and nucleic acids are called **macromolecules**. They are composed of smaller molecules.

The dry mass of living organisms is in the form of carbohydrates, lipids, proteins and nucleic acids.

Water is a good **solvent** capable of dissolving a wide range of chemical substances. This includes all ions and molecules with charged groups. Ions are charged and are surrounded by shells of water; water clusters around the charged groups of glucose and amino acids. This is shown in Figure 2.

A **solute** dissolves in a **solvent** to form a **solution**. Ions and charged molecules (solutes) are surrounded by water (solvent) and so are separated into solution.

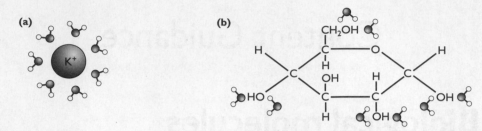

Figure 2 (a) K^+ with a shell of water molecules; (b) glucose with clusters of water molecules

Knowledge check 1

Explain how water acts as a solvent. What type of molecules will not dissolve in water?

The biochemical reactions within the cell are carried out in solution. (Since the water content of seeds and spores is as low as 10% their biochemical activity is suspended until they become rehydrated.) Water is also used to transport nutrients and waste substances.

The hydrogen bonding of water molecules is known as **cohesion**. This is an important property in the flow of a continuous column of water (and dissolved nutrients) through the xylem vessels of plants. You will study this in AS Unit 2.

Knowledge check 2

What type of energy can break hydrogen bonds easily?

Water also has an important role in temperature regulation since evaporation of water from a surface cools it down. The energy required to break the hydrogen bonding in liquid water is known as the **latent heat of evaporation**.

Since **ions** are soluble in water this is the way in which living organisms absorb certain elements. The atoms contained within the ion have specific roles (see Table 1).

Table 1 The role of ions and their atoms as components of biologically important molecules

Ion	Chemical symbol	Role in biological molecule
Nitrate	NO_3^-	Nitrogen in the amino group of amino acids and in the organic base of nucleotides produced in plants
Sulfate	SO_4^{2-}	Sulfur in the R group of the amino acid cysteine
Phosphate	PO_4^{3-}	In a range of important molecules: adenosine triphosphate, ATP; nucleotides and so nucleic acids; phospholipids
Calcium	Ca^{2+}	In calcium pectate, which contributes to the middle lamella of plant cell walls; in calcium phosphate in the bones of vertebrate animals
Magnesium	Mg^{2+}	In the chlorophyll molecule
Iron	Fe^{3+}	In the haemoglobin molecule

Since ions and polar molecules (e.g. glucose and amino acids) are charged and have shells or clusters of water, this influences how they pass through cell-surface membranes (see p. 48).

Carbohydrates

Carbohydrates contain carbon, hydrogen and oxygen. They have the general formula $C_x(H_2O)_y$. The simplest carbohydrates are single sugars (**monosaccharides**) with the formula $(CH_2O)_n$, where n can vary from 3 to 9. The important types of monosaccharide are **trioses** (n = 3), **pentoses** (n = 5) and **hexoses** (n = 6). Two hexose sugars bond together to form a **disaccharide** (double sugar) via a **condensation** reaction (a chemical reaction in which two molecules are joined together and one molecule of water is removed). **Polysaccharides** are formed when many hexose sugars are linked by condensation reactions. Disaccharides and polysaccharides release hexose sugars via **hydrolysis**.

Important monosaccharides include:
- the pentose sugars, **ribose** and **deoxyribose** — these are constituents of nucleotides that form the nucleic acids RNA and DNA
- the hexose sugars, α-glucose, β-glucose and fructose (see Figure 3)

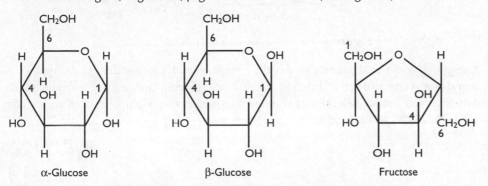

Figure 3 α-glucose, β-glucose and fructose

The carbon 1, carbon 4 and carbon 6 positions are indicated in the glucose molecules shown above. These are important since it is at these positions that different glucose molecules bond together. The subtle but important distinction between α-glucose and β-glucose is that the –H and –OH groups at the carbon 1 position are reversed. This means that the two types of glucose bond slightly differently.

The hexose sugars can bond together to produce disaccharides:
- α-glucose and fructose form **sucrose** — sucrose (cane sugar) is the form in which carbohydrates are transported in plants
- α-glucose and α-glucose form **maltose** — the product of starch digestion

The formation of maltose is a **condensation reaction** since water is removed in the process. The bond formed is an **α-1,4-glycosidic bond** (see Figure 4). Note that the two α-glucose molecules are not in the same plane. The breaking of a glycosidic bond is a **hydrolysis reaction**. In this case, maltose would be hydrolysed to its constituent α-glucose molecules. The formation and hydrolysis of maltose is shown in Figure 4.

Knowledge check 3

A heptose is a monosaccharide with seven carbon atoms. One example is sedoheptulose, which is produced during photosynthesis. What is its molecular formula?

Examiner tip

Be careful not to confuse the terms 'maltose' and 'maltase'. The ending '-ose' tells you that the molecule is a carbohydrate; the ending '-ase' tells you that the molecule is an enzyme. Maltase is the enzyme that catalyses the hydrolysis of maltose.

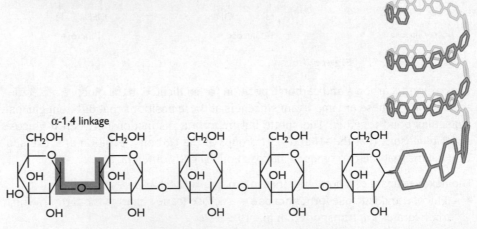

α-Glucose

α-Glucose

Condensation

Hydrolysis

H_2O

H_2O

Maltose

Note that the bond causes the α-glucoses to lie at different angles

α-1,4-glycosidic bond

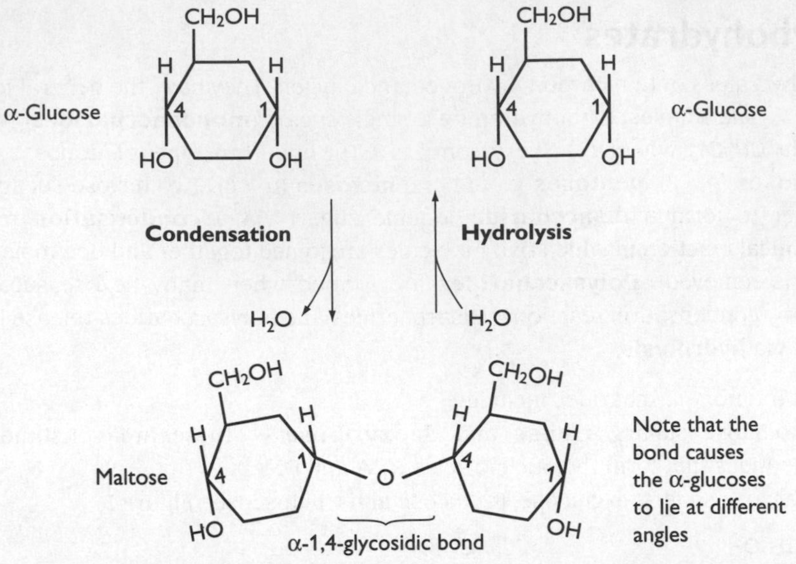

Figure 4 The formation and hydrolysis of maltose

A condensation **polymer** is a substance of many similar units. The basic units are known as **monomers**. All polysaccharides are polymers of monosaccharides, e.g. glucose.

Many α-glucose molecules can bond to produce polysaccharides. The simplest is **amylose**, a constituent of starch in plants (see Figure 5). Only α-1,4-glycosidic bonds are involved and a helical structure results since the α-glucoses join at slightly different angles to each other.

α-1,4 linkage

CH_2OH CH_2OH CH_2OH CH_2OH CH_2OH

OH   OH   OH   OH   OH

HO

OH   OH   OH   OH   OH

Figure 5 The structure of amylose

Knowledge check 4

Starch molecules from different plants differ from each other. Identify two ways in which they may be different.

Two other polysaccharides are produced when **α-1,6-glycosidic bonds** are added at regular intervals to produce branches. In **amylopectin**, also a constituent of starch, α-1,6 bonds occur every 24 to 30 glucose units; in **glycogen**, found in the liver and muscle cells of mammals α-1,6 bonds occur every 8 to 10 glucose units, resulting in more frequent branching. The structure of a branched polysaccharide is shown in Figure 6.

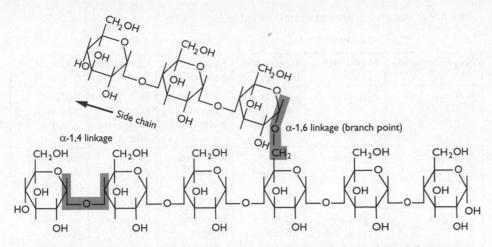

Figure 6 The structure of a branched polysaccharide: amylopectin and glycogen

Glucose is an important respiratory substrate. The polysaccharides amylose and amylopectin in starch, and glycogen, are the means by which glucose is stored in organisms (so they are regarded as energy stores). They are well adapted as storage molecules because:

- many glucose molecules can be stored in a cell (amylose molecules are coiled and so compact)
- they are readily hydrolysed to release glucose molecules (especially amylopectin and glycogen, which are branched and so have many terminal ends for the hydrolytic enzymes to act)
- they are insoluble and so cannot move out of cells
- they are osmotically inert (only soluble substances affect the water potential of a cell — see pp. 46–47)

Many β-glucose molecules bond to produce the polysaccharide **cellulose**. Due to the way in which the β-glucose molecules are orientated cellulose molecules are straight chains. Adjacent cellulose molecules are linked by hydrogen bonds and grouped to produce **microfibrils**. Each microfibril consists of hundreds of cellulose molecules and is a structure of immense tensile strength. Cellulose microfibrils mesh to form the **cell wall** of the plant cell and prevent the cell from bursting in dilute solutions. The structure of cellulose is shown in Figure 7.

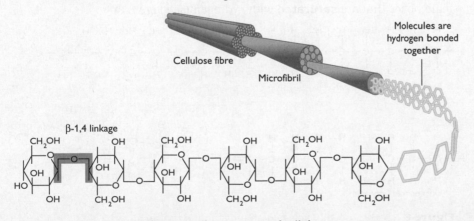

Figure 7 The structure of cellulose

> **Knowledge check 5**
>
> Glycogen is significantly more branched than amylopectin. Explain how this difference is important in animals, which have a much greater metabolic rate than plants.

Knowledge check 6

Give two structural differences between amylose and cellulose.

Some polysaccharides are compared in Table 2.

Table 2 A summary of different polysaccharides

Polysaccharide	Monomer	Glycosidic bond(s)	Shape of polymer	Location	Function
Amylose	α-glucose	α-1,4 bonds only	Unbranched, helical molecule	Starch grains in living plant cells	Store of glucose (energy)
Amylopectin	α-glucose	α-1,4 and 1,6 bonds	Branched, helical molecule	Starch grains in living plant cells	Store of glucose (energy)
Glycogen	α-glucose	α-1,4 and 1,6 bonds	Branched, helical molecule	Granules in liver and muscle cells of mammals	Store of glucose (energy)
Cellulose	β-glucose	β-1,4 bonds only	Straight chains cross-linked to parallel chains	Cell walls of plant cells	Structural support to plant cell

Lipids

Lipids contain mostly carbon and hydrogen with a few atoms of oxygen; they may contain other types of atom. They are macromolecules, but they are not polymers. They are a diverse group structurally, the common feature being their insolubility in water. They can be extracted from cells by organic solvents. Examples include triglycerides (fats and oils), phospholipids, steroids (e.g. cholesterol) and waxes.

Fatty acids are an important constituent of triglycerides and phospholipids. They are essentially long hydrocarbon chains with a carboxylic acid group at one end. They can vary according to:

- the length of the hydrocarbon chain
- whether the hydrocarbon chain contains double bonds — a hydrocarbon with double bonds is described as **unsaturated** in comparison with chains with only single bonds that are **saturated** with hydrogen (see Figure 8)

Examiner tip

Be careful not to confuse the terms 'fatty acid' and 'fat'. A fatty acid is one product of lipid hydrolysis; a fat is a lipid in solid form.

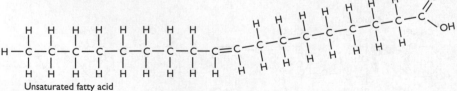

Figure 8 A saturated fatty acid and an unsaturated fatty acid with one double bond

Triglycerides consist of a **glycerol** molecule bonded by condensation reactions to three fatty acids. **Ester bonds** are formed. The constituent molecules of a triglyceride are released by hydrolysis reactions. The formation and hydrolysis of a triglyceride are shown in Figure 9.

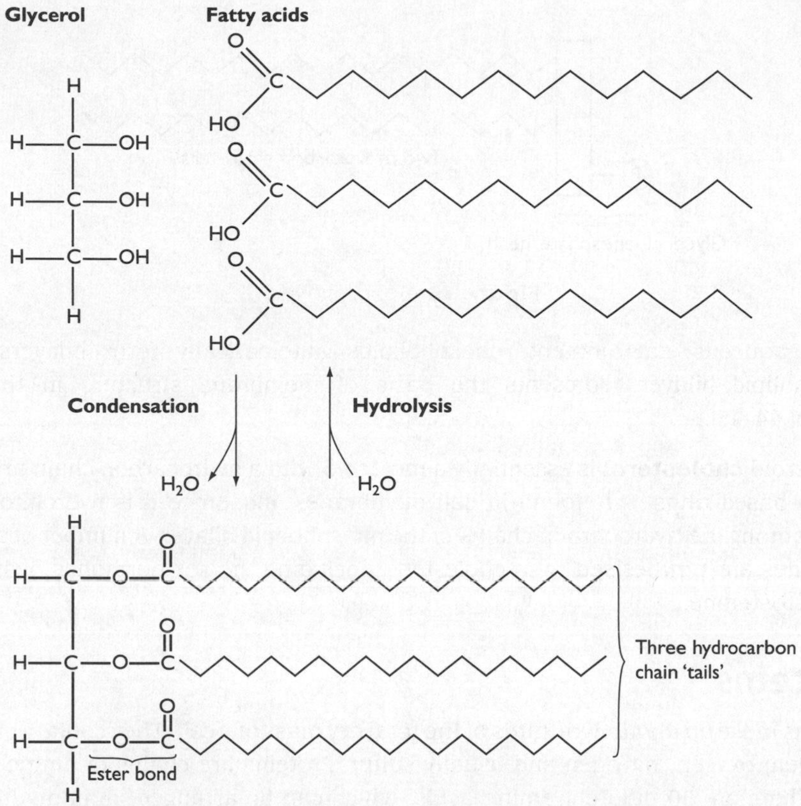

Knowledge check 7

Triglycerides are large molecules formed by condensation reactions but are not condensation polymers. Explain why triglycerides are not polymers.

Figure 9 The formation and hydrolysis of a triglyceride

Triglycerides with unsaturated hydrocarbon chains (or with shorter chains) have lower boiling points than those with saturated hydrocarbon chains. Therefore:

- triglycerides with unsaturated hydrocarbon chains tend to be liquid at room temperatures — oils
- triglycerides with saturated hydrocarbon chains are solid — fats

Oils tend to be found in plants while fats occur in animals.

Like polysaccharides, triglycerides represent energy stores (particularly the constituent fatty acids). They represent an efficient means of storing energy since gram-for-gram they release more energy that carbohydrate. As a mass-efficient means of storing energy, lipids are found in seeds (e.g. linseed oil), migratory birds (e.g. ducks) and in the camel's hump. Fats are also important in providing:

- a thermal insulating layer in mammals, since they are poor heat conductors
- buoyancy in marine mammals such as dolphins and whales
- a cushioning layer around, and therefore protection to, internal organs such as the kidneys

Fatty acids may only be respired aerobically.

Examiner tip

The initial letters SSS and DUL are useful memory aids: SSS — **S**ingle (bonds), **S**aturated (triglyceride), **S**olid (at room temperature); DUL — **D**ouble (bonds), **U**nsaturated (triglyceride), **L**iquid (at room temperature).

A **phospholipid** consists of a glycerol molecule, two fatty acid residues and a phosphate group (see Figure 10). The phosphate causes the glycerol end (the 'head') to be polarised and, therefore, soluble in water (**hydrophilic** or 'water-loving'); the long hydrocarbon chains (the 'tails') are non-polar and insoluble in water (**hydrophobic** or 'water-hating').

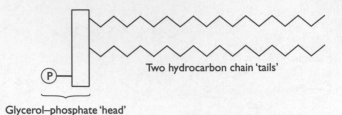

Two hydrocarbon chain 'tails'

Glycerol–phosphate 'head'

Figure 10 A phospholipid

In an aqueous environment, phospholipids automatically form bilayers. The phospholipid bilayer represents the basis of membrane structure in the cell (see pp. 44–45).

The steroid **cholesterol** is essentially a molecule with a hydrocarbon chain and four carbon-based rings. It is found in cell membranes and, since it is hydrophobic, is found among the hydrocarbon chains of the phospholipid bilayer. A number of steroid hormones are synthesised from cholesterol, including the sex hormones oestrogen and testosterone.

Proteins

Proteins make up about two-thirds of the total dry mass of a cell. They contain carbon, hydrogen, oxygen, nitrogen and usually sulfur. Proteins are chains of amino acids. Since there are 20 different amino acids, which can be arranged in many different sequences, a huge variety of proteins is possible. Proteins have a highly organised structure with up to four levels of organisation. The overall shape is precise and integral to the function of the protein in the cell.

Amino acids consist of a carbon atom with four groups attached:

- an amino group
- a carboxylic acid group
- a hydrogen atom
- a residue (R-group)

It is the residue that differs to form the 20 different naturally occurring amino acids. Some of the residues carry a charge and so may be involved in hydrogen bonding, some are hydrophobic and a few contain sulfur (e.g. cysteine). The general structure of an amino acid is shown in Figure 11.

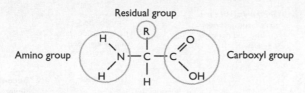

Figure 11 The general structure of an amino acid

Amino acids can bond together to form a **dipeptide**. A condensation reaction is involved and the amino acids are linked by a **peptide bond**. A hydrolysis reaction breaks the dipeptide down to release the two amino acids. The formation and hydrolysis of a dipeptide are shown in Figure 12.

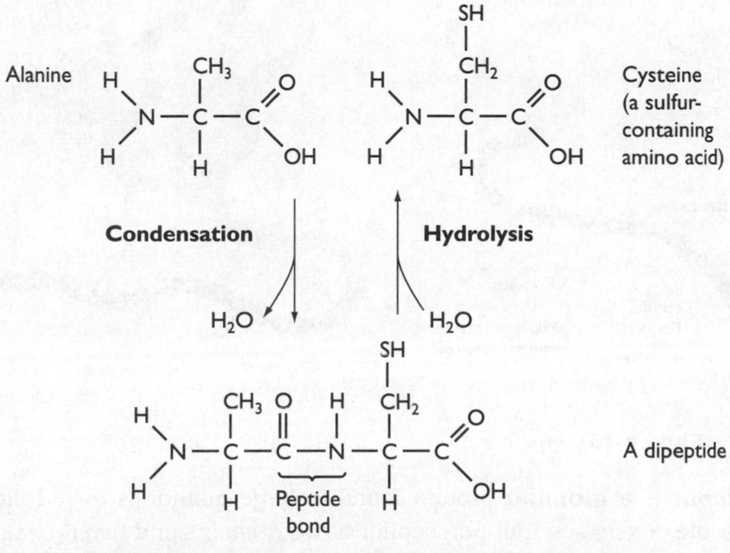

Figure 12 The formation and hydrolysis of a dipeptide

Many amino acids are peptide bonded together to form a **polypeptide**. The **primary structure** of a polypeptide is the sequence of amino acids in the chain. The polypeptide has an amino group at one end and a carboxyl group at the other.

The **secondary structure** is either an α-helix or a β-pleated sheet. The structures are held in place by hydrogen bonds between peptide links in adjacent parts of the chain.

Globular proteins have a **tertiary structure**. The polypeptide folds over on itself in a precise way to produce a specific three-dimensional shape. This is due to interaction between the free R-groups of the amino acids. Different R-groups produce specific links with each other: hydrogen bonds between polar R groups; hydrophobic interactions between non-polar R-groups; ionic bonds between ionised R-groups; disulfide bonds between the sulfur-containing R-groups of cysteine residues. A different order of amino acids means that the R-group interactions are different and so a different three-dimensional shape is generated. Fibrous proteins lack a tertiary structure.

Some proteins consist of two or more polypeptide chains bonded together. This is the **quaternary structure**.

The levels of organisation in a protein molecule are shown in Figure 13.

Examiner tip

With the exception of a generalised amino acid, you will not be asked to draw molecular structures from scratch. However, you may be required to recognise structures, or complete diagrams of carbohydrates, lipids or protein molecules, or their constituents.

Covalent bonds are formed when two atoms share one or more electrons. In proteins, peptide bonds and disulfide bonds are examples of covalent bonds. Covalent bonds are stronger than hydrogen bonds.

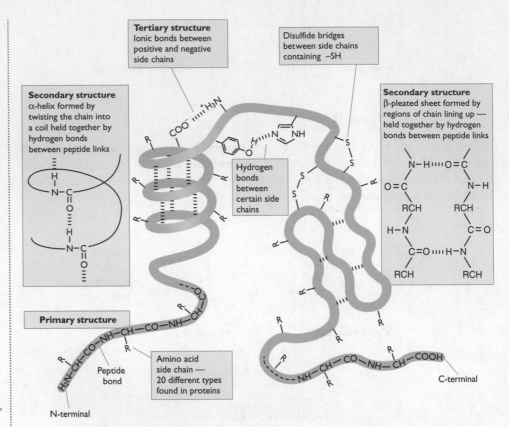

Knowledge check 9

List the type(s) of bonds that form each of the following levels of protein structure: primary structure, secondary structure and tertiary structure.

Figure 13 The different levels of structure in a protein molecule

Haemoglobin is a **globular** protein found in large quantities in red blood cells. Each molecule consists of four polypeptides: two α-chains and two β-chains (Figure 14). Each polypeptide has an iron-containing haem group attached. Haemoglobin is important in the transport of oxygen in animals. An oxygen molecule can associate with each haem to form oxyhaemoglobin.

Collagen is a **fibrous** protein. Each molecule consists of three identical polypeptides coiled round each other and held together by hydrogen bonds (Figure 14). Collagen molecules are bonded together to form the strong fibres found in the skin, tendons and ligaments.

Knowledge check 10

Describe the similarities and differences between haemoglobin and collagen.

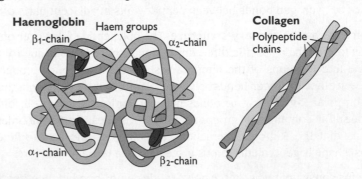

Figure 14 Haemoglobin and collagen are proteins with a quaternary structure

Conjugated proteins have a non-protein part attached. The non-protein component is called a **prosthetic** group. Some conjugated proteins are given in Table 3.

Table 3 Some important conjugated proteins

Name	Prosthetic group	Location
Glycoprotein	Carbohydrate	Mucin (component of saliva); cell-surface membrane
Lipoprotein	Lipid	Membrane structure
Nucleoprotein	Nucleic acid	Chromosome structure; ribosome structure
Haemoglobin	Haem (iron-containing)	Red blood cells

Examiner tip

As a part of your revision, construct a list of definitions for all the terms shown in bold (or in the margins) within this chapter. This is an exercise that you should complete for each of the following chapters.

Practical work

Use biochemical tests to detect the presence of carbohydrates and proteins:
- iodine test
- Benedict's test
- Clinistix
- Biuret test

Carry out paper chromatography of amino acids:
- preparation, running and development of the chromatogram
- calculation of R_f values

Summary

- Water molecules are bipolar. They are attracted to each other and surround ions and molecules with charged groups, which are thus dissolved by the water.
- A range of ions is required for the synthesis of many biological molecules.
- Carbohydrates consist of monosaccharides (single sugars), disaccharides and polysaccharides.
- Monosaccharides are classified according to the number of C atoms: pentose (5C) sugars, e.g. ribose and deoxyribose; hexose (6C) sugars, e.g. α-glucose, β-glucose and fructose.
- Disaccharides include: maltose formed from two α-glucose molecules; sucrose formed from an α-glucose and a fructose.
- The polysaccharides amylose and amylopectin (forming starch in plants) and glycogen (in animals) are stores of α-glucose molecules (which are used in respiration to release energy). The bonds between the α-glucose molecules are 1,4-glycosidic bonds though amylopectin and glycogen have, in addition, 1,6-glycosidic bonds, which cause them to branch.
- Cellulose is a polysaccharide of β-glucose. Straight chains are formed that H-bond with each other to provide fibres of high tensile strength in plant cell walls.
- Triglycerides are lipids composed of three fatty acids joined to a glycerol by ester bonds.
- Fatty acids can be either saturated or unsaturated (in which case there is a double bond in the hydrocarbon chain). Fatty acids release energy in aerobic respiration.
- A phospholipid consists of glycerol bonded to two fatty acids and a phosphate. The glycerol-phosphate end is hydrophilic (water soluble) while the hydrocarbon chains are hydrophobic (water insoluble).
- Amino acids are joined by peptide bonds to form polypeptides. There are 20 different amino acids and, since any number can be joined in any order, an infinite variety of polypeptides is possible.

Summary

- Polypeptides form the basis of protein structure. Proteins have different levels of structure: primary structure (sequence of amino acids); secondary structure (α-helix or β-pleated sheet); tertiary structure (folding of polypeptide into a globular shape); and quaternary structure (with two or more polypeptide chains).
- The formation of glycosidic, ester and peptide bonds to build up macromolecules involves condensation reactions; their breakdown involves hydrolysis reactions.

Knowledge check 11

Which of the following enzyme-controlled reactions in plant cells is anabolic and which is catabolic?

(a) the formation of maltose from starch

(b) the synthesis of starch from glucose-1-phosphate

Enzymes

The chemical reactions of an organism are collectively called **metabolism**. Metabolic reactions include:

- **catabolism** — 'breakdown' reactions
- **anabolism** — 'build-up' reactions

Enzymes catalyse metabolic reactions — there is one type of enzyme for each reaction.

The theory of enzyme action

In order to catalyse a reaction, the enzyme and substrate must first collide to form an **enzyme–substrate complex**. Catalysis then takes place on the enzyme surface, according to the equation below:

$$E + S \rightarrow ES \rightarrow EP \rightarrow E + P$$

Enzyme + substrate → Enzyme–substrate complex → Enzyme–product complex → Enzyme + product

The enzyme is unchanged at the end of the reaction (and the same products are formed whether the reaction is catalysed or uncatalysed).

The reaction takes place on a particular part of the enzyme molecule called the **active site**. In an anabolic reaction, the substrate molecules are orientated in such a way on the active site as to allow bonding between them. In a catabolic reaction, the formation of the active site round the substrate assists the breaking of a particular bond. In both cases the enzyme functions as a catalyst by effectively lowering the **activation energy** required for the reaction to take place. This reduction in activation energy is illustrated in Figure 15.

Knowledge check 12

What is the 'activation energy' of a reaction?

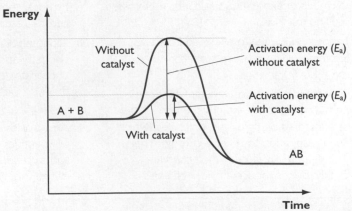

Figure 15 The effect of a catalyst on the activation energy of a reaction

CCEA AS Biology

Enzymes are **specific**. For any one type of reaction there is a particular enzyme required for catalysis — if there are 1000 different kinds of reaction in a cell, then the cell contains 1000 different types of enzyme.

There are two models to explain how enzymes work:
- the **lock-and-key** model (see Figure 16)
- the **induced-fit** model (see Figure 17)

The lock-and-key model of enzyme action proposes that the active site of an enzyme has a complementary shape (like a lock) into which the substrate molecule (the key) fits exactly, to form the enzyme–substrate complex. The induced-fit model suggests that initially, the shape of the active site is not quite complementary to that of the substrate, but as the substrate begins to bind, the active site changes shape and 'moulds' itself around the substrate molecule (like a glove fitting round a hand). The induced-fit model is considered more useful because it better explains the way in which activation energy is reduced in catabolic reactions.

Knowledge check 13

Explain the specificity of enzymes.

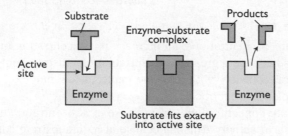

Figure 16 The lock-and-key model of enzyme action

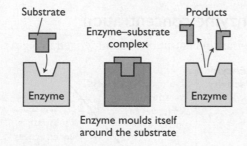

Figure 17 The induced-fit model of enzyme action

Properties of enzymes

A number of external factors influence the activity of enzymes and, therefore, the rate of biological reactions. These include substrate concentration, enzyme concentration, temperature and pH.

There are two key points to remember when explaining these influences:
- Enzyme molecules need to collide with substrate molecules, so factors that influence the chance of collision, such as substrate concentration and temperature, influence the rate of reaction.

Examiner tip
You should understand how enzymes reduce activation energy in both anabolic and catabolic reactions. For anabolic reactions, the substrate molecules are held on the active site and orientated in such a position as to facilitate bonding between them. For a catabolic reaction, the binding of the substrate induces a conformational change in the shape of the active site that distorts the substrate molecule, so facilitating the breaking of a particular bond.

- Enzymes are globular proteins with a precise tertiary structure, so factors that influence protein shape or the binding of the substrate, such as high temperature and pH, influence the rate of reaction.

The effect of substrate concentration on enzyme activity

The influence of substrate concentration is summarised in Figure 18.

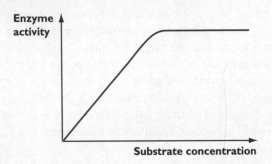

Figure 18 The effect of substrate concentration on enzyme activity

- At low substrate concentrations, an increase in concentration increases enzyme activity. This is because a greater concentration of substrate molecules increases the chances of collision with enzyme molecules. Therefore, more enzyme–substrate complexes are formed.
- At high substrate concentrations, an increase in concentration does not cause a further increase in activity. This is because at high substrate concentrations the enzymes are fully employed and so, at any one moment, all the active sites are occupied.

The effect of enzyme concentration

The influence of enzyme concentration is summarised in Figure 19.

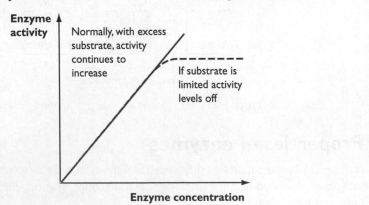

Figure 19 The effect of enzyme concentration on enzyme activity

An increase in enzyme concentration increases the rate of reaction. At high enzyme concentration activity may level off, but only if there is insufficient substrate. This is because an increase in the concentration of enzyme molecules increases the chance of successful collisions with substrate molecules. (There is normally only an incline phase since enzymes are used over-and-over again and so function efficiently at very low concentrations.)

The effect of pH on enzyme activity

The influence of pH is summarised in Figure 20.

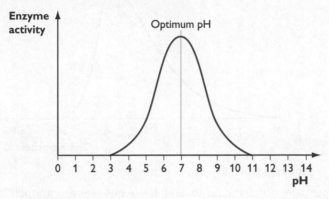

Figure 20 The effect of pH on enzyme activity

Enzyme activity is at a maximum at the optimum pH. An increase or decrease in pH causes a decrease in enzyme activity (Figure 21). This is because the structure of the protein and, therefore, the active site of the enzyme are altered by changes in pH. In particular, ionic bonds in the tertiary structure may be disrupted. So at non-optimal pH, the substrate attaches less readily to the enzyme and there is a specific pH at which the bonding possibilities at the active site best facilitate the formation of an enzyme–substrate complex.

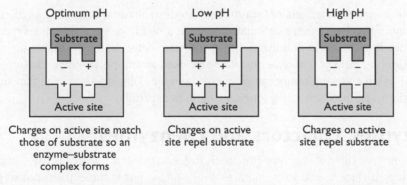

Figure 21 The effect of pH

The effect of temperature on enzyme activity

The influence of temperature is summarised in Figure 22.

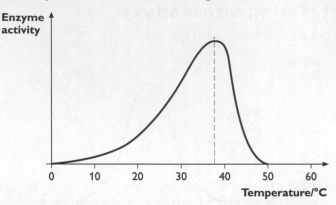

Figure 22 The effect of temperature on enzyme activity

- At low temperatures, an increase in temperature causes an exponential increase in enzyme activity — typically, a 10°C rise in temperature doubles the rate of reaction. This is because an increase in temperature provides more kinetic energy for the collision of enzyme and substrate, so the rate of formation of enzyme–substrate complexes increases.
- At high temperatures (typically above 40°C), an increase in temperature causes a sharp decline in enzyme activity. This is because at higher temperatures, the hydrogen bonds and ionic bonds holding the tertiary structure of the enzyme molecules are broken and so the active site loses its complementary shape for substrate attachment — the enzyme is denatured.

Not all enzymes have an optimum temperature of around 40°C. Enzymes from organisms that live in very cold habitats have a much lower optimum temperature. Enzymes from bacteria that live in hot springs are active at temperatures up to 90°C. For example, the DNA polymerase enzyme used in the polymerase chain reaction (PCR) has an optimum temperature of 80°C and was obtained from the thermophilic bacterium *Thermus aquaticus*, found living in hot springs.

Enzymes, cofactors and coenzymes

Some enzymes do not function effectively unless a non-protein **cofactor** is attached. Cofactors include metal ions, such as Mg^{2+}, and organic molecules (**coenzymes**) that are often derivatives of vitamins. Cofactors function either by influencing the shape of an enzyme (to its optimum for substrate attachment) or by participating in the enzymatic reaction (by attaching to one of the products for transfer to another enzyme). Some examples of cofactors and coenzymes are given in Table 4.

Table 4 Examples of cofactors and coenzymes

Enzyme	Cofactor	Role of enzyme
Carbonic anhydrase	Zinc ion (Zn^{2+})	Catalyses the combination of CO_2 with water to form carbonic acid in red blood cells, facilitating the transport of CO_2 in the blood
Cytochrome oxidase — a respiratory enzyme	Copper ion (Cu^{2+})	Combines electrons and hydrogen ions with oxygen in respiration
Enzyme	**Coenzyme**	**Role of enzyme and coenzyme**
Pyruvate decarboxylase — a respiratory enzyme	Coenzyme A	Pyruvate (3-carbon molecule) is broken down to acetate, which is 'picked up' by coenzyme A (forming acetyl CoA), and CO_2, which diffuses out of the cell
Succinate dehydrogenase — a respiratory enzyme	FAD (derived from vitamin B2, riboflavin)	Hydrogen is removed from succinate and 'picked up' by FAD (to form $FADH_2$)

Knowledge check 16

Chloride is a cofactor of amylase, the enzyme that catalyses the breakdown of starch to maltose molecules. What would happen to the production of maltose if amylase had to function in the absence of chloride ions?

Examiner tip

The examples shown in Table 4 are provided only to illustrate the roles of cofactors and coenzymes. You do not need to learn these — most are involved in respiratory metabolism, which is covered in A2 Unit 2.

Enzyme inhibitors

Enzyme inhibitors are molecules that bind to enzymes and decrease their activity.

- A **competitive inhibitor** closely resembles the structure of the substrate and so competes for the active site, but does not remain there permanently (see Figure 23).

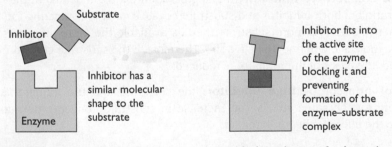

Figure 23 A competitive inhibitor competes with the substrate for the active site

- A **non-competitive inhibitor** does not resemble the substrate and may act in different ways:
  - inhibitor molecules bind to other parts of the enzyme away from the active site, altering the overall shape of the enzyme molecule, including the active site (see Figure 24); the inhibitor may leave the enzyme so that the active site regains its catalytic shape
  - inhibitors bind to parts of the enzyme molecule, leaving the enzyme permanently damaged; some (e.g. cyanide, CN⁻) combine irreversibly at the active site

Inhibitors may be described as 'competitive' or 'non-competitive' and as 'reversible' or 'non-reversible (permanent)'. These terms may cause confusion. You should remember that:

- competitive inhibitors are always reversible
- non-competitive competitors may be reversible or permanent
- non-reversible inhibitors are always non-competitive

Knowledge check 17

Heavy metal ions, such as mercury (Hg⁺), silver (Ag⁺) and arsenic (As⁺), alter the tertiary structure of a protein by breaking its disulfide bonds. What type of enzyme inhibitor would they be?

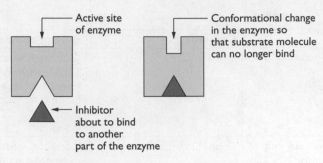

Figure 24 One type of non-competitive inhibitor

The effects of both types of inhibitor on enzyme activity at increasing substrate concentration are shown in Figure 25.

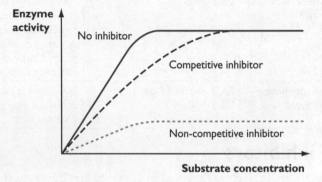

Figure 25 The effect of substrate concentration on enzyme activity in the presence of a competitive inhibitor and a non-competitive inhibitor

Effect of competitive inhibitor: the degree of inhibition depends on the relative concentration of both inhibitor and substrate because each is competing for a place on the active site. The more substrate there is available the more likely it is that a substrate molecule will find an active site. Therefore, if the substrate concentration is increased, the effect of the inhibitor is reduced.

Effect of non-competitive inhibitor: the substrate and the inhibitor are not competing for the same site, so an increase in substrate concentration does not decrease the effect of the inhibitor.

Some examples of enzyme inhibitor are shown in Table 5.

Table 5 Examples of enzyme inhibitors

Enzyme	Inhibitor	Type
Succinate dehydrogenase — a respiratory enzyme	Malonate — similar in structure to succinate (the substrate)	Competitive inhibitor (reversible)
Cytochrome oxidase — a respiratory enzyme	Potassium cyanide, KCN — combines with the active site	Non-competitive inhibitor (and irreversible)

Immobilised enzymes

An immobilised enzyme is an enzyme that is attached to an inert, insoluble material. Methods of immobilisation include:

- adsorption — the enzyme is attached to the outside of an inert material such as porous glass
- covalent bonding — the enzyme is bonded onto a solid such as cellulose
- cross-linkage — a binding chemical (e.g. glutaraldehyde) is used to cross-link the enzyme
- encapsulation — the enzyme is confined within a selectively permeable membrane, e.g. nylon
- entrapment — the enzyme is trapped inside a gel, e.g. alginate beads

Enzyme immobilisation facilitates the use of continuous-flow column reactors (see Figure 26).

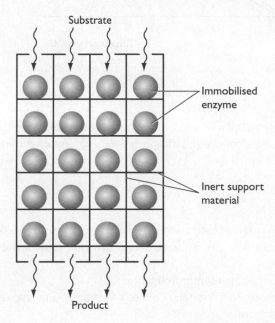

Figure 26 Immobilised enzymes in a continuous-flow column reactor

Immobilisation provides advantages in the commercial use of enzymes:

- The product is enzyme-free.
- The enzyme can be re-used.
- Since the enzyme is supported, its stability is improved. This means that it remains active over a greater range of pH and temperatures (thermostability) than would be the case if the enzyme were in solution (see Figure 27).

However, immobilisation can reduce enzyme activity:

- The active site of the immobilised enzyme may be blocked by the support matrix (adsorption).
- Insoluble substances may hinder the arrival of the substrate (entrapment).
- The active site may be altered during the binding process (cross-linkage).

Using the graph in Figure 27, list three differences between the effects of temperature on the immobilised enzyme and on the free enzyme.

Further, the flow rate through the column influences activity. If it is too slow the reaction is completed early in the column; too fast and not all the substrate will have been engaged in the reaction.

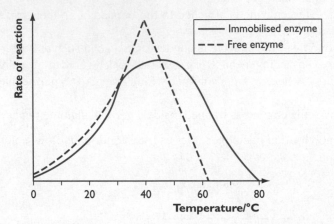

Figure 27 The effect of temperature on free enzyme (in solution) and immobilised enzyme

Examiner tip

A graphical-skills question may ask you to 'plot the results, using an appropriate graphical technique'. You will have decisions to make: What type of graph is most appropriate? What is the most appropriate caption? Which is the independent variable? Graphical presentation of results is dealt with in greater detail in the CCEA Unit 3 guide.

Uses

Immobilised enzymes have a variety of commercial uses. Enzymes can be immobilised onto reagent dip-strips for diagnostic purposes, e.g. the enzymes glucose oxidase and peroxidase on Clinistix.

Practical work

Carry out experimental investigation of factors affecting enzyme activity:
- effect of temperature, pH, substrate and enzyme concentration on enzyme activity
- demonstration of enzyme immobilisation
- use of a colorimeter to follow the course of a starch–amylase reaction (or other appropriate reaction)

Summary

- The chemical reactions within an organism represent its metabolism. Each metabolic reaction involves a substrate being converted to a product and is catalysed by an enzyme.
- Catalysts speed up the rate of reaction by lowering the activation energy required for the reaction to occur.
- Enzymes are globular proteins with a specific tertiary shape, part of which forms an active site.
- A substrate binds with the active site to form an enzyme–substrate complex. Products are formed at the active site. The products are

released from the enzyme molecules, which are unaltered.
- There are two models of enzyme action: the lock-and-key hypothesis and the induced-fit hypothesis.
  - The lock-and-key hypothesis explains enzyme specificity, due to the complementary shape of the substrate and the enzyme's active site.
  - The induced-fit hypothesis suggests that binding of the substrate induces a change in enzyme structure which, through putting the substrate molecule under tension, explains why activation energy is lowered in catabolic reactions.

- Factors that increase the rate at which substrate and enzyme molecules might collide will increase the rate of reaction and include temperature, substrate concentration and enzyme concentration.

- Factors that affect the tertiary structure of the enzyme will have an adverse effect on enzyme action by preventing binding of the substrate and include high temperatures and pH changes away from the optimum.

- Cofactors are non-protein substances that are necessary for the actions of some enzymes. Cofactors can be ions or organic molecules (coenzymes).

- Inhibitors are substances that reduce the activity of enzymes:
  - Competitive inhibitors mimic the substrate and compete with it for the enzyme's active site; the extent of the inhibition depends on the relative proportion of substrate and inhibitor molecules.
  - Non-competitive inhibitors tend to stop enzyme activity and act in different ways.

- Enzymes can be immobilised in a variety of ways and provide many advantages for their commercial use.

Nucleic acids

Nucleic acids are macromolecules composed of chains of nucleotides. They carry coding information and are found in all living cells and viruses. There are two forms: **deoxyribonucleic acid** (**DNA**) and **ribonucleic acid** (**RNA**).

The role of DNA is the long-term storage of genetic information:
- It is the means by which genetic information is passed from generation to generation. It is able to do this because it is capable of **self-replication**.
- It acts as a **code**, since it contains the instructions needed to construct other cell components, such as proteins and RNA. The code on DNA is represented by the sequence of bases in the nucleotides.

Lengths of DNA that carry the genetic information for the synthesis of proteins are called **genes**. Genes consist of nucleotides with a specific sequence of bases. The sequence of the bases determines the sequence of amino acids in a polypeptide, coding for the order in which amino acids are brought together.

RNA molecules assist the functioning of DNA. They retrieve information from DNA and direct the synthesis of proteins. RNA molecules act as messengers between DNA in the nucleus and the sites of protein synthesis (the ribosomes) in the cytoplasm. They also form portions of the ribosomes and serve as carrier molecules for amino acids to be used in protein synthesis.

Nucleotide structure

Nucleotides are the subunits of nucleic acids. Each nucleotide (see Figure 28) consists of:
- a **pentose** sugar — **deoxyribose** or **ribose**
- a **nitrogenous base** — from **adenine**, **guanine**, **cytosine** and **thymine** (in deoxyribonucleotides only) or **uracil** (in ribonucleotides only)
- a **phosphate** group (attached to the carbon-5 of the sugar)

Knowledge check 19

The components of a nucleotide are bonded by condensation reactions. How many molecules of water are produced during the formation of a nucleotide?

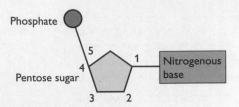

Figure 28 A generalised nucleotide (the numbers indicate the position of carbon atoms in the 5-carbon sugar)

Deoxyribonucleotides and ribonucleotides are compared in Table 6.

Table 6 A comparison of deoxyribonucleotides and ribonucleotides

Feature	Deoxyribonucleotides	Ribonucleotides
Pentose sugar	Deoxyribose	Ribose
Nitrogenous base	Adenine (A), guanine (G), cytosine (C), thymine (T)	Adenine (A), guanine (G), cytosine (C), uracil (U)
Macromolecule formed	DNA	RNA

Nucleic acid structure

Nucleotides join together by condensation reactions forming **phosphodiester bonds** (between the phosphate of one nucleotide and the C3 of the pentose of the other nucleotide) along a 'sugar–phosphate' backbone. The polynucleotide strand formed has a free **5′-end** (with phosphate attached) and a free **3′-end**. This is illustrated in Figure 29.

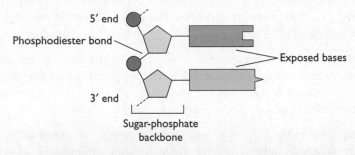

Figure 29 The basic structure of a polynucleotide

Knowledge check 20

In a nucleic acid polymer, which component parts are at the ends of the molecule?

Knowledge check 21

Define the term 'anti-parallel'.

A DNA molecule consists of **two anti-parallel strands**. The bases on opposite strands are joined by hydrogen bonds in a precise way: adenine always bonds with thymine; guanine always bonds with cytosine (see Figure 30). This is known as base pairing.

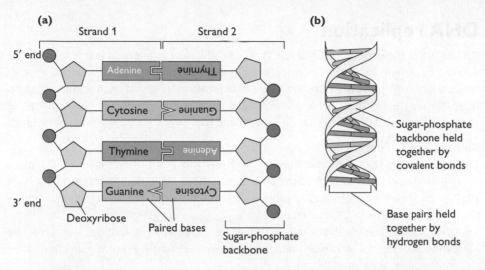

Figure 30 (a) The structure of DNA; and (b) formed into a double helix

The nucleotides join at slightly different angles to each other and so the whole structure forms a **double helix**; the hydrogen bonding between the two strands increases its stability.

RNA molecules are single stranded and are much shorter than DNA molecules — DNA may be millions of nucleotides long, RNA usually consists of a few hundred nucleotides. There are three forms of RNA:

- **Messenger RNA (mRNA)** carries the code for the synthesis of a polypeptide from the DNA in the nucleus to a ribosome where the polypeptide is assembled.
- **Transfer RNA (tRNA)** carries the amino acids to the ribosome to be used in polypeptide synthesis. tRNA is single stranded and folded into a clover-leaf shape, with hydrogen bonding within the folds.
- **Ribosomal RNA (rRNA)** forms part of the structure of ribosomes. These organelles are the sites at which polypeptides are assembled.

DNA and RNA are compared in Table 7.

Table 7 A comparison of DNA and RNA

Feature	DNA	RNA
Subunits	Deoxyribonucleotides (contains deoxyribose and thymine)	Ribonucleotides (contains ribose and uracil)
Length	Very long	Relatively short
Types	One (though nucleotide sequences differ)	Three: mRNA; tRNA; rRNA
Strands	Double stranded	Single stranded (though tRNA and rRNA have folds that are bonded)
Base pairing	A with T and G with C	No base pairing (except joining folds within tRNA and rRNA)

Examiner tip

If you are given the percentage of one base in a DNA molecule, you can readily calculate the percentages of the remaining bases. For example: if the bases of a DNA are 30% thymine, and adenine pairs with T, then there must be 30% A; and since the remaining 40% must be shared equally by cytosine and guanine (since they base pair) then there is 20% C and 20% G.

Examiner tip

Be careful to distinguish the terms nucleotide and nucleic acid. For example, you could be asked to list differences between deoxyribonucleotides and ribonucleotides or between deoxyribonucleic acid and ribonucleic acid. There are more differences between DNA and RNA than between their constituent nucleotides — compare Tables 6 and 7.

DNA replication

Since DNA is the genetic code for the synthesis and development of whole organisms, it must be copied exactly from one generation to the next. This is achieved by self-replication, using a **semi-conservative mechanism** in which each strand acts as a template for the synthesis of a new strand. Each new DNA molecule contains one of the original strands in addition to a new strand (hence the name semi-conservative).

The sequence of events in DNA replication is as follows:

(1) The enzyme DNA helicase breaks the hydrogen bonds holding the base pairs together and 'unzips' part of the DNA double helix, revealing two strands.

(2) The enzyme DNA polymerase moves along each strand, which acts as a template for the synthesis of a new strand.

(3) DNA polymerase catalyses the joining of free deoxyribonucleotides to each of the exposed original strands, according to base pairing rules, so that new complementary strands form.

(4) The process of unzipping and joining new nucleotides continues along the whole length of the DNA molecule.

Each DNA molecule so formed is identical to the other and to the original DNA (and contains one strand of the original).

DNA replication is illustrated in Figure 31.

Examiner tip

Learn the base pairing rules: A–T, C–G. It is common to ask students to write out the complementary sequence to a given DNA sequence.

Knowledge check 22

What is the sequence of bases on the complementary strand created by replication of a 'parental' strand with the sequence ATCTGTA?

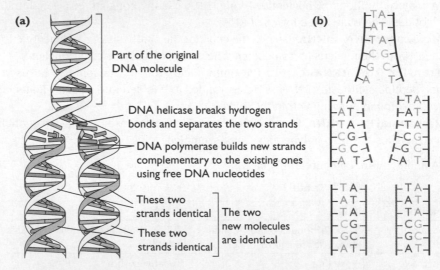

Figure 31 (a) DNA replication; (b) semi-conservative replication of DNA

The evidence for semi-conservative replication: Meselson and Stahl's experiment

Experimental evidence that DNA replicates semi-conservatively came from a classic experiment devised by Matthew Meselson and Franklin Stahl in 1958. They grew bacteria (*Escherichia coli*) in a medium in which nitrogen was supplied (in ammonium ions) in the form of the heavy, but non-radioactive, isotope, ^{15}N. Consequently, the DNA of the bacteria became entirely heavy.

These bacteria were then transferred to a medium containing the normal (light) isotope, ^{14}N. Immediately before changing the medium and then at intervals corresponding to successive generations, samples of bacteria were removed and the DNA was extracted.

Analysis of the extracted DNA involved density-gradient centrifugation, a technique that separates molecules of different molecular masses; heavier molecules are deposited at a lower level in the centrifuge tube. The results were as predicted by the semi-conservative hypothesis. Immediately before the change of medium, the DNA occupied a single band corresponding to 'heavy' DNA. After one generation the DNA was of 'intermediate' density, being concentrated in a single band a little higher up the tube. This is to be expected if all the DNA molecules consist of one heavy strand and one light strand. After two generations there were two bands, with 50% of the DNA 'intermediate' and 50% 'light'. The results and their interpretation are shown in Figure 32.

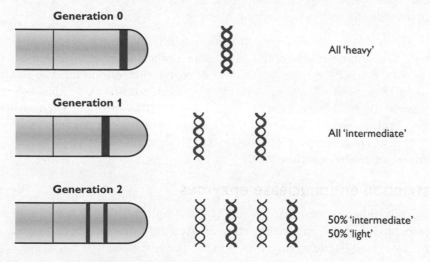

Figure 32 Meselson and Stahl's experiment

Knowledge check 23

Work out the proportions of light and intermediate DNA in the third generation. Use Figure 32 to help you.

The genetic code

A **gene** is a length of DNA that codes for a protein (polypeptide). The protein may be structural (e.g. collagen) or functional (e.g. membrane proteins and enzymes). Since proteins control the activities of organisms, the genes ultimately determine their characteristics.

Humans possess about 30 000 genes, which represents only 10% of the total DNA. Between the genes there are extensive non-coding regions of DNA, the function of which is uncertain.

The order of bases on one strand of the length of DNA that forms the gene determines the order by which amino acids are sequenced during the formation of a polypeptide. The bases are 'read' in triplets (triplet code). Each triplet of bases acts as a code for a specific amino acid (just as '● ● ●' is the Morse code for the letter 's') — for example:

Bases in the DNA strand:	ATG	GCT	GAA	TGT
Amino acid sequence:	methionine	alanine	glutamate	cysteine

Examiner tip

At AS you are not expected to have knowledge of protein synthesis. The process by which proteins are synthesised is dealt with in detail in A2 Unit 2.

DNA technology

The nucleotide sequence of our DNA determines the essence of our being. The nucleotide sequences of our genes (the coding regions) determine the proteins that we produce. The nucleotide sequences of the non-coding regions, while not well understood, are highly variable, which makes them valuable in determining how closely related two individuals might be. The ability to study the base sequences of DNA allows a number of interesting questions to be tackled:

- Does a particular gene differ from person to person?
- Is an allele (a particular form of a gene) associated with a hereditary disease?
- Are two persons closely related; are two DNA samples the same?
- How much does the DNA of individuals within a population vary; how much genetic diversity is there within a particular species?
- How much does the DNA of different species vary; how can this be used to unravel the taxonomic relationships among species?

Determining the similarities and differences in the nucleotide sequences of DNA samples is possible because of the development of a number of tools. For example, one genetic marker site relies on the use of **restriction endonuclease** enzymes, obtained from certain bacteria. The recognition of specific nucleotide sequences in different DNA fragments relies on the use of **DNA probes**; **DNA profiling** (**fingerprinting**) is used to compare the DNA of individuals. If the initial sample for analysis does not contain sufficient DNA, then the amount can be amplified using the **polymerase chain reaction** (**PCR**).

Restriction endonuclease enzymes

Restriction endonuclease enzymes cut DNA at specific nucleotide (base) sequences. Bacteria produce these enzymes to counter attack by viruses (bacteriophages). They do this by cutting bacteriophage DNA into smaller, non-infectious fragments.

There are many different restriction enzymes produced by different species of bacteria. Each enzyme cuts DNA at a specific base sequence — the recognition (or restriction) site (see Table 8). The enzymes may make staggered cuts in the DNA, commonly called **sticky ends**.

Table 8 Some examples of restriction endonuclease enzymes

Restriction endonuclease	Bacterial origin	Recognition site
EcoRI	E. coli	G A A T T C C T T A A G
HindIII	H. influenzae	A A G C T T T T C G A A
BamHI	B. amyloliquefaciens	G G A T C C C C T A G G

The enzyme cuts the DNA producing a particular number of fragment lengths depending on the number of recognition sites in the DNA — if there are four sites then five fragment lengths are produced.

Restriction endonuclease enzymes have been used to establish restriction fragment length polymorphisms (see below) and may be used in DNA profiling.

Knowledge check 24

In a particular length of DNA, the recognition site for the restriction endonuclease enzyme *Eco*RI exists five times. How many different DNA fragments will be produced?

Examiner tip

The use of restriction endonuclease enzymes in obtaining DNA fragments to use in gene transfer (genetic engineering) is dealt with in A2 Unit 2.

Genetic markers

A genetic marker is a nucleotide sequence that is variable within a population and can, therefore, be used to measure differences between individuals. Three genetic markers are described:

- **Restriction fragment length polymorphisms** (RFLPs — pronounced riflips). The different array of fragment lengths produced when a specific restriction endonuclease enzyme is used to cut different DNA molecules. The variation is due to differences in the number of recognition sites between individuals.
- **Microsatellite repeat sequences** (MRSs). Short runs of simple two-, three-, or four-base sequences found within the non-coding regions of the DNA, which are therefore highly variable. The number of repeats of these microsatellites (e.g. CCTA) varies between individuals and the pattern of MRSs within the DNA of an individual is unique. It is MRSs that are analysed in DNA profiling (fingerprinting).
- **Single nucleotide polymorphisms** (SNPs — pronounced snips). These are differences in single nucleotides among samples of DNA molecules. SNPs within genes are particularly interesting since they may indicate the cause of a genetic disease. For example, a single nucleotide change in the gene that codes for the β-chain of haemoglobin causes sickle-cell anaemia. In this disease, the red blood cells are distorted and the haemoglobin is less effective at carrying oxygen.

Knowledge check 25

What type of genetic marker is indicated by the DNA base sequence ATATATATAT? How would this marker differ in different individuals?

The polymerase chain reaction (PCR)

The polymerase chain reaction (PCR) mimics the natural process of DNA replication. It can generate billions of copies of a DNA sample within a few hours. It is also possible to select particular sections of DNA to replicate — for example, sections containing microsatellite repeat sequences (in DNA profiling).

The process requires:

- a DNA sample that includes the selected region for replication
- the synthesis of primers — short strands of DNA (of about 20 nucleotides) that are complementary to the sequence at the start of each strand of the region to be amplified
- the enzyme DNA polymerase, extracted from thermophilic bacteria and which is therefore thermostable
- free deoxyribonucleotides

The sequence of events in PCR (see Figure 33) is as follows:

(1) The DNA to be amplified (copied many times) is heated to 95°C. This breaks the hydrogen bonds and separates the two strands.

(2) The mixture is cooled to 53°C, which allows the primers to bind to the start of each strand of the selected DNA region. The primers prevent the DNA strands rejoining and act as signals to the polymerase enzymes to start adding nucleotides.

(3) The mixture is heated to 73°C and the thermostable polymerase enzyme copies each strand, starting at the primers.

(4) The process is repeated and with each cycle the number of DNA molecules is doubled — a chain of 20 cycles would produce millions of copies of the original DNA.

The technique is used by forensic scientists and archaeologists to study small samples of DNA, and may be used in DNA profiling.

Knowledge check 26

The enzyme most commonly used in the PCR is **Taq DNA polymerase** extracted from the bacterium *Thermus aquaticus* (see page 22). This enzyme is described as 'thermostable' because it is not denatured at temperatures up to 80°C. Explain why it is important that the DNA polymerase used in the PCR is thermostable.

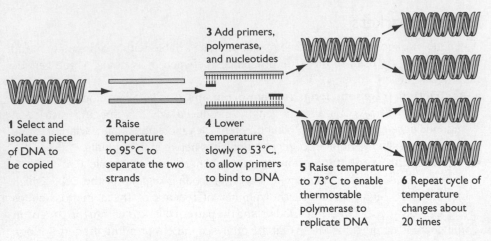

Figure 33 Stages in the polymerase chain reaction (PCR)

The DNA probe

A DNA probe is used to locate a particular section of DNA. It consists of a short length of single-stranded DNA with a specific nucleotide (base) sequence. The probe binds by base pairing to a complementary region of single-stranded target DNA. In order to be able to detect the probe and the target DNA to which it is attached, the probe is either radioactive or fluorescent. Detection takes place using an X-ray film for radioactive probes or a laser scanner for a fluorescent probe.

DNA profiling (fingerprinting)

The DNA of the genes that code for the proteins of an individual does not show much variation. This is because differences to the nucleotide sequences would be mutations and could result in non-functional proteins. However, the vast amount of non-coding ('junk') DNA that exists between the genes is highly variable. Within the non-coding regions, **microsatellite repeat sequences** are found. A microsatellite (e.g. CCTA) may be repeated between five and 15 times.

DNA profiling uses MRSs that are very similar between closely related individuals but so variable that unrelated individuals are extremely unlikely to have the same MRSs.

One method of DNA profiling makes *use of restriction endonuclease to cut sections of DNA containing the MRSs*:

- The DNA is treated with a specific restriction endonuclease to cut the DNA into fragments either side of the MRSs. If there are a large number of repeats then the fragment will be long; if there are few repeats small fragments will be produced.
- The fragments of DNA are separated by gel electrophoresis on the basis of size — smaller fragments move further.
- The bands are heated to make them single stranded, transferred (blotted) to a nylon membrane (Southern blotting) and washed with DNA probes that are complementary to the microsatellite region.
- This is repeated using several probes for different MRSs and the resulting fragments are detected.
- Only those DNA fragments that have bound to the labelled probe show up — the resulting pattern of bands is called a DNA fingerprint and looks rather like a bar code.

Knowledge check 27

Distinguish between a 'DNA primer' and a 'DNA probe'.

This technique is illustrated in Figure 34.

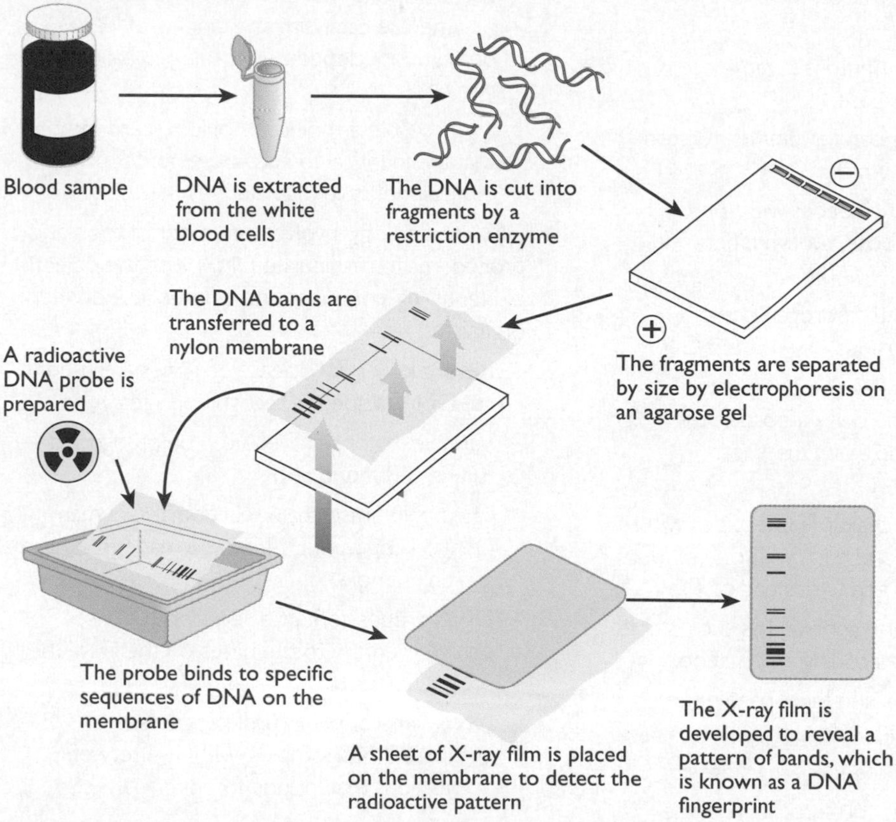

Blood sample

DNA is extracted from the white blood cells

The DNA is cut into fragments by a restriction enzyme

The DNA bands are transferred to a nylon membrane

A radioactive DNA probe is prepared

The fragments are separated by size by electrophoresis on an agarose gel

The probe binds to specific sequences of DNA on the membrane

A sheet of X-ray film is placed on the membrane to detect the radioactive pattern

The X-ray film is developed to reveal a pattern of bands, which is known as a DNA fingerprint

Figure 34 Stages in preparing a DNA profile (genetic fingerprint) using restriction endonuclease

Examiner tip
Remember that each individual has unique DNA giving a unique pattern of bands. In the examination, you may be asked to compare DNA fingerprints. You can only conclude that an individual's DNA is present in a sample found at, say, a crime scene if *all* the bands are included. Also, a child's DNA will produce bands some of which will be found in the mother while the father must possess *all* those remaining.

Another method (presently used by the UK Forensic Science Service) makes *use of the polymerase chain reaction to amplify the MRSs*:

- Fluorescent DNA primers that will attach next to the region containing the MRSs are synthesised.
- PCR is used to replicate large numbers of DNA fragments containing the MRSs. This allows minute quantities of source material to be analysed.
- The fragments of DNA produced by PCR are separated using gel electrophoresis.
- This is completed for ten different microsatellites, each four bases in length, with an additional primer for determining gender.
- The position of the DNA fragments is revealed as a pattern of fluorescent bands due to the fluorescent tags on the DNA primers flanking the microsatellite regions. The bands are detected using a laser scanner.
- The results are displayed in a graph of fluorescence against fragment size — the DNA profile.

DNA profiling is a powerful tool in forensic science, in settling paternity disputes, in establishing kinship, and in studying the genetic diversity of species and the evolutionary relationship between taxonomic groups.

Knowledge check 28

Explain why forensic scientists often use PCR when producing a genetic fingerprint.

Summary

- DNA and RNA are nucleic acids, which are polymers of nucleotides.
- A nucleotide consists of a pentose sugar, a phosphate and an organic base.
- DNA consists of two anti-parallel strands, twisted to form a double helix, in which:
  - each strand contains nucleotides with the pentose sugar deoxyribose, though differing in the organic base — A, T, C or G
  - specific base pairing, with hydrogen bonds, occurs between the strands — A–T and C–G
  - phosphodiester bonds join the phosphate of one nucleotide to the deoxyribose of the neighbouring nucleotide along the 'sugar-phosphate backbone'
- RNA is a single-stranded chain of nucleotides with the pentose sugar ribose and each with one of four organic bases — A, C, G and U (instead of T).
- DNA is the molecule of the gene and as such is able to self-replicate and carries coding information.
- RNA exists as three types and takes part in the interpretation of the DNA code.
- DNA replication involves the following stages:
  - DNA helicase catalyses the separation of the two strands.
- Each strand forms a template with DNA polymerase catalysing the binding of free deoxyribonucleotides according to base-pairing rules.
- Two complete molecules of DNA are formed that are identical to each other and to the original molecule of DNA.
- DNA technology involves a number of tools and procedures to manipulate DNA with the object of identifying similarities and differences between organisms:
  - Restriction endonuclease enzymes are used to cut DNA at specific recognition sites.
  - Variable regions of DNA can be recognised — RFLPs, MRSs and SNPs
  - The polymerase chain reaction allows many identical copies of DNA to be made from a small starting sample.
  - DNA probes contain a sequence of bases complementary to the bases on the DNA being sought.
  - DNA fingerprinting (profiling) is used to compare DNA samples, with a variety of applications that include forensic analysis.

Cells and viruses

The cell is the structural unit of all living organisms. Many living organisms consist of just a single cell, while others are composed of many cells. These multicellular organisms possess cells that are adapted to perform specialised functions (e.g. mesophyll cells in a leaf for photosynthesis and epithelial cells in the ileum for absorption). Nevertheless, there are many functions that all cells undertake (e.g. ATP synthesis, protein synthesis) and so they possess common features within their internal structure.

There are two categories of cell: **prokaryotic** and **eukaryotic**. The prokaryotic cells lack the degree of 'compartmentalisation' that eukaryotic cells possess — they lack a nucleus and other membrane-bound organelles. Bacteria are prokaryotes. Eukaryotes include animals, plants and fungi.

Viruses are not cells and are not themselves living. They have an intimate relationship with, and reproduce in, living cells.

Microscopy and cell ultrastructure

Two types of microscope are used in the study of cells: the **light microscope** and the **electron microscope**. Both **magnify** the fine structure of an object. However, **resolution** is even more important. This is the ability to discriminate fine detail so that two neighbouring points are seen as separate, rather than as a larger blur. The electron microscope has much greater resolving power than the light microscope because electrons have a shorter wavelength than light. The light microscope has its advantages, one of which is that living processes, such as mitosis, can be viewed. The interior of an electron microscope is a vacuum and so specimens must be dead. These two types of microscope are compared in Table 9.

Table 9 A comparison of the light microscope and the transmission electron microscope

Light microscope	Transmission electron microscope
Uses light: wavelength 450–700 nm	Uses electrons: wavelength 0.01 nm
Light refracted by glass lenses	Electron beams refracted by electromagnetic lenses
Low resolution: 200 nm	High resolution: 0.1 nm
Low magnification: ×1500 maximum	High magnification: ×1 000 000 maximum
Image formed on the retina of the eye or recorded on photographic film	Image formed on a fluorescent screen or recorded on photographic film
Limited in cellular detail that is revealed	Limited to dead specimens and by the likelihood of artefacts (deviations from the 'real' appearance as a result of the treatment of the specimen in preparation for microscopy)
Advantage: can be used to view living cells	Advantage: produces high-resolution images of cells and organelles

The **scanning electron microscope** (SEM) is similar to the **transmission electron microscope** (TEM) except that the specimen is coated in a film of gold and electrons are reflected off the surface to create a three-dimensional effect image.

Skills development

Numeracy skills — magnification

The specimen viewed using a microscope is called the **object**. It is increased in size by a certain **magnification** and presented in a micrograph as the **image**. The image, or a *scale bar* on the micrograph, can be measured so that knowing either the true (actual) size of the object, or the magnification, allows the other to be calculated. The magnification of a micrograph is calculated as:

$$\text{magnification} = \frac{\text{measured size of image}}{\text{true size}}$$

Examiner tip

Remember that the main advantage of the electron microscope over the light microscope is *not* just that it provides a greater magnification but that it greatly increases the resolution — the ability to discern fine detail.

Examiner tip

The advantage of the light microscope in being able to view living cells is important. For example, it allows the action of a phagocyte or the process of mitosis to be seen.

Examiner tip

Students often get confused with the conversion of units. You should *measure* the object on the micrograph in millimetres (mm). Then a simple multiplication by 1000 presents the length in micrometres (μm).

The true size of an object (e.g. an organelle) is calculated as:

$$\text{true size} = \frac{\text{measured size of image}}{\text{magnification}}$$

Of course, all *measurements must be in the same units*. The conversion factors are as follows:

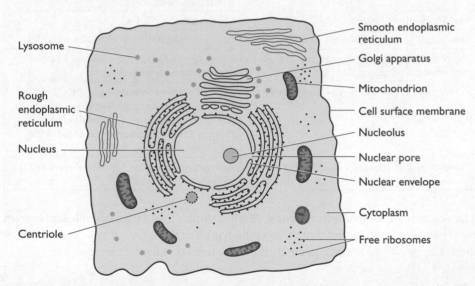

The eukaryotic cell

The appearance of a cell viewed via an electron microscope is its **ultrastructure**. The ultrastructure of a generalised animal cell is shown in Figure 35.

Eukaryotes also include plants and fungi. Their cells have some distinctive features (see Figure 36 — cells not drawn to scale).

Figure 35 The ultrastructure of an animal cell

CCEA AS Biology

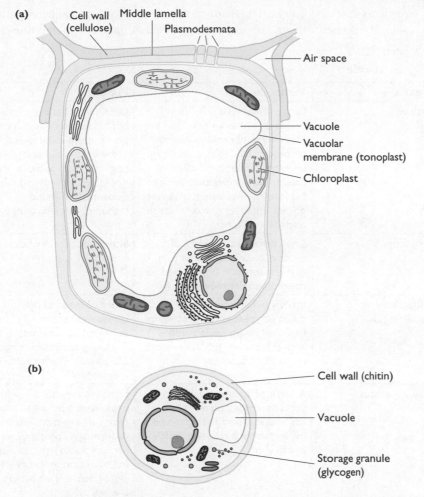

(a)
Cell wall (cellulose)
Middle lamella
Plasmodesmata
Air space
Vacuole
Vacuolar membrane (tonoplast)
Chloroplast

(b)
Cell wall (chitin)
Vacuole
Storage granule (glycogen)

Figure 36 Distinctive features of (a) a plant cell; (b) a fungal cell

Both plant and fungal cells have cell walls, though made of different materials. The cell wall prevents the cell bursting when in dilute solution.

Animal, plant and fungal cells are compared in Table 10.

Table 10 A comparison of animal, plant and fungal cells

Animal cell	Plant cell	Fungal cell
No cell wall	Cellulose cell wall	Chitin cell wall
No chloroplasts	Chloroplasts	No chloroplasts
Glycogen granules (carbohydrate (energy) store)	Starch grains (carbohydrate (energy) store)	Glycogen granules (carbohydrate (energy) store)
Lysosomes	No lysosomes	Lysosomes
No permanent vacuole	Large central vacuole	Vacuole
Centrioles	No centrioles (except mosses and ferns)	No centrioles (except one group)
No plasmodesmata	Plasmodesmata	No plasmodesmata

Examiner tip

In exams you are often presented with a photomicrograph of cells. You should be able to identify organelles in micrographs. Past papers containing micrographs are available on the CCEA website to allow ample practice.

Knowledge check 30

List (a) three features present in a plant cell but not found in an animal cell and (b) three features present in a fungal cell but not found in a plant cell.

The structures that perform particular functions within a cell are called **organelles** (see Table 11). Some of these are surrounded by membranes — membrane-bound organelles.

Table 11 The structure and function of eukaryotic cell organelles

Organelle	Structure	Function
Nucleus	Largest organelle (10–30 µm) enclosed within an envelope (double membrane); contains chromosomal DNA which may be extended (euchromatin) or condensed (heterochromatin); perforated envelope (possesses pores); contains one or several nucleoli (1–2 µm)	DNA codes for the synthesis of proteins in the cytoplasm; pores in the envelope allow large molecules in (e.g. enzymes) and out (e.g. RNA); nucleolus synthesises ribosomal RNA and manufactures ribosomes
Ribosomes	Small bodies (20–25 nm) of protein and rRNA either free in the cytoplasm or attached to rough endoplasmic reticulum	Site of protein synthesis
Endoplasmic reticulum (ER)	Membrane system of sacs and tubes permeates the cytoplasm; flattened rough ER is studded with ribosomes; tubular smooth ER lacks ribosomes	Proteins made in the ribosomes accumulate in the rough ER and are passed onto the Golgi apparatus; smooth ER is involved with lipid metabolism
Golgi apparatus	A stack of membrane-bound sacs (cisternae); forming face has vesicles from the rough ER joining; mature face has vesicles pinching off	Dynamic structure in which proteins are modified (may have carbohydrate attached to form glycoproteins) and packaged into vesicles either for secretion by exocytosis or for delivery elsewhere in the cell
Lysosomes	Vesicles produced by the Golgi apparatus which contain hydrolytic enzymes	Lysosomes combine with membrane-bound degenerate organelles or ingested particles (e.g. bacteria) to form secondary lysosomes; hydrolytic enzymes digest the contents (see Figure 37)
Mitochondria (singular: mitochondrion)	Sausage-shaped (1 µm wide and up to 10 µm long); surrounded by an envelope, the inner membrane of which is folded to form cristae; fluid-filled matrix; several to thousands per cell	Synthesis of ATP by aerobic respiration
Chloroplasts	Ovoid (2–10 µm in diameter); surrounded by an envelope; elaborate internal membrane system of lamellae with thylakoids stacked into grana; contain lipid droplets and starch grains; occur in some plant cells	Site of photosynthesis; chlorophyll molecules are attached to the lamellae

Knowledge check 31

The following are functions of different organelles. Name the organelles in each case: (a) synthesis of lipids; (b) produces ATP through aerobic respiration; (c) production of spindle microtubules during nuclear division.

Knowledge check 32

Name the organelle in each case that possesses the following structures: (a) cisternae; (b) cristae; (c) thylakoids.

Knowledge check 33

What cellular processes would be taking place in a cell with: (a) much rough endoplasmic reticulum; (b) a prominent Golgi body; (c) a cell-surface membrane convoluted to form many microvilli?

Table 11 The structure and function of eukaryotic cell organelles (*continued*)

Organelle	Structure	Function
Vesicles and vacuoles	Bound by a single membrane; vesicles are much smaller than vacuoles; vacuoles are permanent in plant and fungal cells; membrane of the sap vacuole in plant cells is called the tonoplast	Vesicles may be used for storage and transport of substances (e.g. transport to and from the cell-surface membrane or within the cytoplasm); vacuoles are for storage of water and ions
Microtubules	Tubular (25 nm in diameter); formed from the protein tubulin; occur within centrioles (as nine triplets of microtubules in a circular arrangement) and throughout the cytoplasm; animal and fungal cells contain a pair of centrioles	Centrioles form the spindle fibres during cell division of animal and fungal cells; microtubules also form part of the cytoskeleton and allow movement of cell organelles
Plasmodesmata (singular: plasmodesma)	Strands of cytoplasm between neighbouring plant cells that pass through pores in the walls	Facilitate transport of materials between adjacent cells in plants

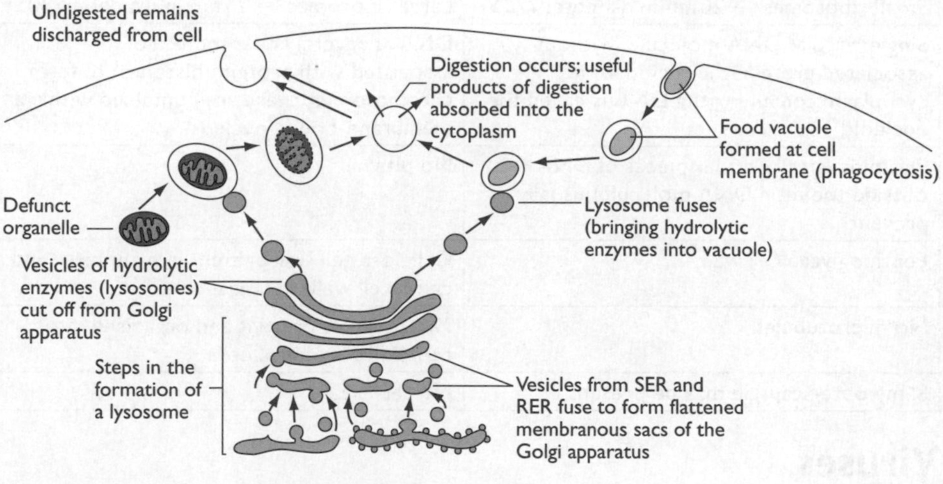

Knowledge check 34

How are the functions of the following organelles linked: (a) nucleolus and ribosomes; (b) rough endoplasmic reticulum, Golgi body and vesicles.

Figure 37 The role of lysosomes

The prokaryotic cell

Prokaryotic cells are particularly small (1–10 μm). They lack a nucleus and other organelles bound by membranes (see Figure 38).

Examiner tip

Students often confuse secretory vesicles and lysosomes. The Golgi apparatus produces *both*. However, their roles are quite distinct. Secretory vesicles are moved to the cell-surface membrane and their contents are exocytosed (see p. 49). Lysosomes remain in the cell where they are involved in intracellular digestion (see Figure 37).

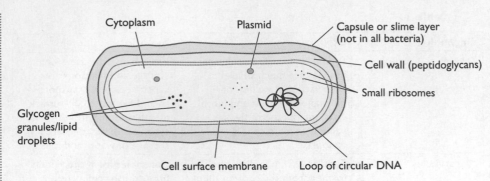

Figure 38 A generalised prokaryotic cell

Prokaryotic and eukaryotic cells are compared in Table 12.

Table 12 Comparison of prokaryotic and eukaryotic cells

Prokaryotic cell	Eukaryotic cell
Small cells — 1–10 μm	Large cells — 10–100 μm
No membrane-bound organelles	Nucleus, mitochondria, endoplasmic reticulum, Golgi apparatus and chloroplasts (in plants) present
Small ribosomes — 20 nm in diameter (70 S)	Large ribosomes — 25 nm in diameter (80 S)
Single circular DNA molecule, without associated protein; the region in the cytoplasm containing the DNA is called the nucleoid	DNA as several linear molecules associated with protein (histones) to form chromosomes; these are contained within a membrane-bound nucleus
Plasmids (small circular pieces of DNA outside the main DNA molecule) usually present	No plasmids
Peptidoglycan cell wall	Cellulose cell wall present in plant cells; and chitin cell walls in fungal cells
No microtubules	Microtubules present and organised into centrioles in animal cells
Slimy outer capsule may be present	No capsule

Viruses

Viruses lack cytoplasm and are not cells. They consist of a nucleic acid core surrounded by a protein coat (capsid). The nucleic acid ultimately acts as a coding device for the production of new viral particles. There are a number of types (see Figure 39).

Examiner tip

Be prepared to make a comparison between a prokaryotic cell and a eukaryotic cell. Make sure that any differences noted are sufficiently distinct. For example, the examiners might regard 'mitochondria absent in prokaryotes' and 'endoplasmic reticulum absent in prokaryotes' as a single point — i.e. 'membrane-bound organelles absent in prokaryotes'.

Knowledge check 35

What are the two main components of a virus particle?

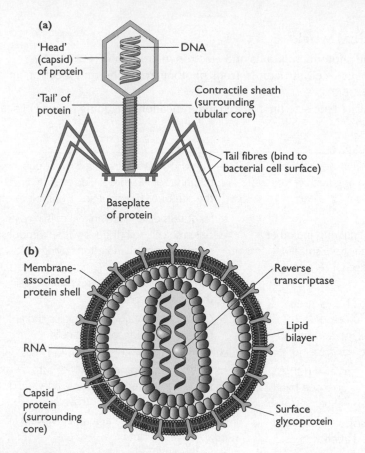

Figure 39 (a) A bacteriophage; (b) The human immunodeficiency virus

Bacteriophages

Bacteriophages (phages) consist of a core of DNA bounded by a protein coat. Phages invade bacteria and the phage DNA codes for the production of new viral proteins (to make new coats). The phage DNA replicates to form many copies which are then packaged in the new protein coats. Eventually the bacterial cells burst to release many new phages.

Human immunodeficiency virus (HIV)

HIV consists of a core of RNA bounded by a protein coat and a lipid bilayer containing glycoproteins. It belongs to a group of viruses containing RNA that are known as **retroviruses**. They contain the enzyme **reverse transcriptase**, which uses the RNA as a template to produce single-stranded DNA; double-stranded DNA is then created with DNA polymerase activity. This viral DNA is integrated into the host DNA where it ensures that viral protein and new copies of RNA are made. HIV invades a type of lymphocyte (helper T-cell) and so may weaken the immune system, thereby causing AIDS — acquired immune deficiency syndrome.

Knowledge check 36

List three differences between viruses and living cells.

Knowledge check 37

A section of the RNA in the HIV has the base sequence AUAUGUACTC. What is the corresponding base sequence on the DNA strand produced by the enzyme reverse transcriptase?

Practical work

Examine photomicrographs and electron micrographs (TEM/SEM):

- Recognise cell structures from photomicrographs and electron micrographs (TEM/SEM).
- Calculate true size (in µm) and magnification, including the use of scale bars.

Summary

- Light microscopes provide magnified views of cells. Electron microscopes produce images with greater magnification and, more importantly, greater resolution.
- Prokaryotic cells (bacteria) lack a nucleus and other membrane-bound organelles; they have smaller ribosomes, a circular loop of naked DNA and a cell wall of peptidoglycan.
- Eukaryotic cells (animals, fungi and plants) are compartmentalised, containing numerous organelles, many of which are membrane-bound, specialising in different metabolic activities.
- The nucleus encloses the genetic material (DNA), contained within chromatin, and is bounded by a perforated nuclear envelope.
- The endoplasmic reticulum consists of sheets of membranes. Rough ER is covered in ribosomes. Smooth ER is the site of lipid synthesis.
- Ribosomes, found on the rough ER or free in the cytoplasm, are the site of protein synthesis.
- The Golgi apparatus consists of a stack of flattened membrane-bound cisternae. It modifies proteins and produces secretory vesicles and lysosomes.
- Lysosomes contain lysozymes and are responsible for intracellular digestion.

- Mitochondria are enclosed by a double membrane, the inner of which is folded to form cristae, and is the site of ATP production by aerobic respiration.
- Plant cells differ from animal cells in having a cellulose cell wall (though with plasmodesmata connecting cells) and often having a sap vacuole. They might also have chloroplasts and lack centrioles, and they possess starch grains rather than glycogen granules.
- Centrioles contain microtubules and are a focus for spindle formation in animal cells.
- Chloroplasts are bounded by an envelope, have internal membranes (lamellae) with thylakoids stacked into grana, and contain the fluid stroma. They are the site of photosynthesis.
- Fungal cells differ in a number of ways from both animal and plant cells.
- Viruses are not cells and only become active within a living host cell. They are able to instruct the cell's metabolism to make new viral particles.
- Viruses consist of a core of nucleic acid and a protein coat (capsid).
  - Bacteriophages (host: bacteria) contain DNA.
  - HIV (host: human helper T-cells) contains RNA and the enzyme reverse transcriptase (producing viral DNA).

Membrane structure and function

The membranes within cells and surrounding them (the cell-surface or plasma membrane) consist of a phospholipid bilayer with associated proteins. In an aqueous environment, phospholipids arrange themselves spontaneously into bilayers so that the hydrophobic 'tail' regions are shielded from the surrounding polar fluid. In cells, this causes the more hydrophilic 'head' regions to associate with the cytoplasmic and extracellular faces on either side.

The structure of the cell-surface membrane

The **phospholipid bilayer** is the basic structure of the cell-surface membrane. There are also **cholesterol** molecules in among the hydrocarbon tails. **Proteins** are attached to the bilayer (**extrinsic**), embedded into one layer (**intrinsic**) or span both layers (**intrinsic** and **transmembranal**). The phospholipids in the cell membrane are constantly moving while the proteins are scattered among them, so that the structure proposed is called the **fluid-mosaic model**.

The membrane also contains **polysaccharides** bound either to the proteins (**glycoproteins**) or to lipids (**glycolipids**). The polysaccharides are on the outer face only, where they form a fringe called the **glycocalyx**.

The fluid-mosaic structure of membranes is illustrated in Figure 40.

Membrane fluidity

A number of factors influence the fluidity of the membrane:

- The more phospholipids with **unsaturated hydrocarbon chains** there are, the more fluid is the membrane. The 'kinks' in the unsaturated hydrocarbon tails prevent them from packing close together so more movement is possible.
- Phospholipids with **longer hydrocarbon chains** will decrease the fluidity of the membrane, since attractive forces among the tails will be greater.
- Fluidity is influenced by **temperature**. The membrane is more fluid at high temperature and less fluid at low temperature as the phospholipid bilayer 'freezes' into a gel (or solid-like) state.
- **Cholesterol** acts as a temperature stability buffer. At high temperature, cholesterol provides additional binding forces and so decreases membrane fluidity. At low temperature, cholesterol keeps the membrane in a fluid state by preventing the phospholipids from packing too close together and 'freezing'.

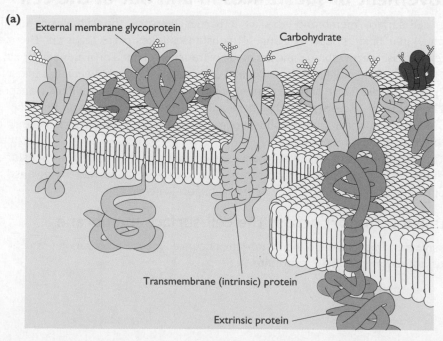

(a)

External membrane glycoprotein

Carbohydrate

Transmembrane (intrinsic) protein

Extrinsic protein

Figure 40 The structure of the cell-surface membrane: (a) a 3D impression

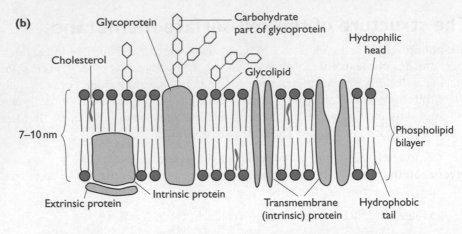

(b)

Figure 40 The structure of the cell-surface membrane: (b) a sectional view

Cell recognition and cell receptors

Glycoproteins and glycolipids have important roles in **cell-to-cell recognition** and as **receptors** for chemical signals. The glycocalyx allows cells to recognise each other and, therefore, group together to form tissues. Glycoprotein receptors and signalling molecules (e.g. hormones) fit together because they have complementary shapes.

Membrane enzymes

Many of the proteins in the membrane are enzymes. The membrane provides the attached enzymes with improved stability (as with immobilised enzymes).

Movement of substances in and out of the cell

The cell-surface membrane acts as a barrier between the cytoplasm and the extracellular fluid, though exchange of substances takes place across it. The route taken to cross the membrane and the mode of transport depend on a number of factors:

- The **size** of the molecule — very small molecules can slip between the phospholipid molecules, large particles can only move in or out by cytosis (bulk transport).
- The **polarity** or **non-polarity** of the substance — non-polar (and lipid-soluble) molecules move through the phospholipid bilayer; polar substances move through the transmembrane proteins.
- The **concentration** of the substance either side of the membrane — substances move from high to low concentration by diffusion; if movement against the concentration is required, then active transport is needed.

Passive transport across the cell-surface membrane

Passive movement through the membrane occurs down a concentration gradient and does not require energy expenditure.

Knowledge check 38

Explain why cell-surface membranes are not all the same.

Knowledge check 39

Suggest why liver and muscle cells are particularly responsive to the hormone insulin.

Examiner tip

You may be asked to explain the route by which polar or non-polar substances can pass across the cell-surface membrane. Remember that polar or water-soluble substances cannot pass through the phospholipid bilayer because of its hydrophobic centre and so must pass via transmembranal proteins. Non-polar or fat-soluble substances are able to pass through the phospholipid bilayer.

Diffusion

Non-polar molecules, such as lipid-soluble vitamins (e.g. vitamins A and D), steroid hormones, the respiratory gases oxygen and carbon dioxide, and very small polar molecules such as water and urea, move through the phospholipid bilayer down their concentration gradients. Ions, which are polar and cannot move through the phospholipid bilayer, and water may diffuse freely through the hydrophilic core of **channel proteins**. These channels have a specific shape to allow only one type of ion through. While some water molecules diffuse through the phospholipid bilayer (since they are so small), most water diffuses through specific water channel proteins called **aquaporins**.

Facilitated diffusion

Carrier proteins may selectively transport ions and molecules with charged groups, such as glucose and amino acids. The substance binds to a site on the protein, which changes shape to bring the substance through the membrane. Movement occurs down the concentration gradient, but being assisted by a carrier is called facilitated diffusion.

Osmosis

Osmosis is the diffusion of water across a differentially permeable membrane (water moves through more easily than solutes). Water moves from an area of higher **water potential** (Ψ) to an area of lower water potential. Pure water (at standard temperature and pressure) is defined as having a water potential of zero. The addition of **solutes** to water lowers its potential (makes it more negative), just as an increase in **pressure** increases its potential (makes it less negative).

water potential of a cell (Ψ_{cell}) = solute potential (Ψ_s) + pressure potential (Ψ_p)

The water potential is a measure of the free energy of the water molecules in a system. The water potential of pure water is zero because all the molecules are 'free'. In solutions, some of the water molecules form shells around the solutes and are, therefore, no longer free (see Figure 41). This lowers the water potential — it becomes negative. Cytoplasm contains solutes, so it has a negative water potential. Therefore, when cells are placed in water, water moves into the cells by osmosis.

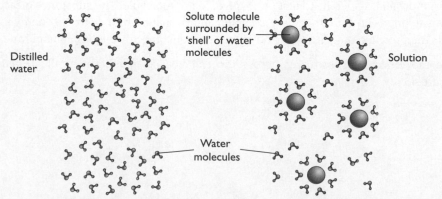

Figure 41 How solutes reduce the water potential of a solution

Knowledge check 43

As water moves into a cell placed in a hypotonic (more watery) solution, what happens to the water potential of the cell?

Examiner tip

You will need to learn the effect of immersing plant and animal cells in either hypotonic or hypertonic solutions.

Examiner tip

Students often lose marks because they do not understand that all cell water potential (and solute potential) values are negative. The highest cell water potential is zero. Therefore the lower the water potential, the more negative it becomes.

Examiner tip

Remember that carrier proteins (in facilitated diffusion or in active transport) have a site that is complementary to, and so is specific to, the substance carried. However, *never* refer to this as the active site — that refers to the binding site on enzymes.

When placed in dilute (hypotonic) solutions, animal cells, such as red blood cells, take up water and swell until they burst (**lyse**). However, the cells of prokaryotes, fungi and plants have rigid walls that prevent them from bursting. The pressure created by the swelling cell increases to a point when water can no longer enter. A swollen plant cell is said to be **turgid**.

When red blood cells are placed in a concentrated (hypertonic) solution, the cells lose water by osmosis, shrink and become **crenated**. In hypertonic solutions, cells with walls also shrink — the cell wall cannot protect them from water loss by osmosis. As they shrink, the cells lose contact with their cell walls. In plant cells, this is known as **plasmolysis** and the point at which the cytoplasm just begins to lose contact with the cell wall is called **incipient plasmolysis**.

Water potential, the solute potential of the cell contents and the pressure potential of a plant cell all change as the cell takes up or loses water osmotically (see Figure 42).

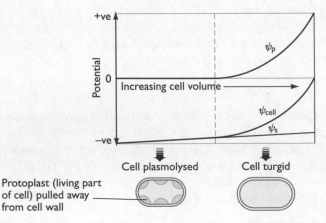

Figure 42 Changes in pressure potential (Ψ_p), solute potential (Ψ_s) and water potential (Ψ_{cell}) of a plant cell as it takes up water osmotically

Active transport across the cell-surface membrane

Active transport causes substances to move across a membrane from a low concentration to a high concentration against the concentration gradient. This requires energy, and the **carrier proteins** involved are referred to as **pumps**. Each carrier protein is specific to just one type of ion or molecule. The substance attaches to a site on the protein (they have complementary shapes) and, with the energy from ATP, the protein changes shape and moves the substance through the membrane.

The movement of substances across the cell-surface membrane is illustrated in Figure 43.

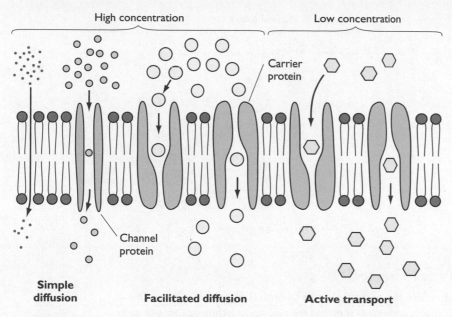

Figure 43 The movement of substances through the cell-surface membrane

Cytosis: bulk transport into and out of the cell

Substances can move into and out of a cell without having to pass through the cell-surface membrane. This involves the bulk transport into the cell (**endocytosis**) or out of the cell (**exocytosis**) of substances too large to be transported by protein carriers.

Endocytosis

During endocytosis the cell-surface membrane invaginates and the membrane folds round the substance to form a vacuole or vesicle that enters the cytoplasm while the cell-surface membrane reforms. There are two main types:

- **Phagocytosis** is the uptake of solid particles into the cell within vacuoles. Examples include the ingestion of bacteria by polymorphs (a type of white blood cell) and the removal of old red blood cells from circulation by the Kupffer cells of the liver.
- **Pinocytosis** is the uptake of solutes and large molecules (such as proteins) into the cell within vesicles.

Exocytosis

During exocytosis, **secretory vesicles** move towards and fuse with the cell-surface membrane, releasing their protein contents out of the cell. Exocytosis is also involved in removal of the waste products of digestion from cells.

Cytosis is illustrated in Figure 44.

Knowledge check 44

State one similarity and one difference between facilitated diffusion and active transport.

Examiner tip

Some questions need you to identify clues from a diagram, a table or a graph about the type of transport that is happening. Look to see if the movement is up or down the concentration gradient and whether ATP is being used.

Knowledge check 45

Why might a cell benefit from microvilli if carrying out active transport?

Knowledge check 46

What term would describe the bulk movement of materials shown by phagocytes?

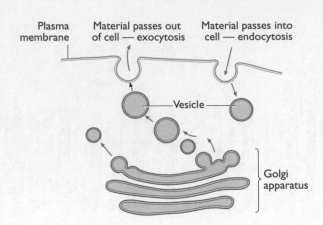

Figure 44 Cytosis: bulk transport

Practical work

Measure the average water potential of cells in a plant tissue:
- use a weighing method for potato or other suitable tissue
- calculate the percentage change in mass
- determine the average water potential from a graph of percentage change in mass against solute potential of immersing solution

Measure the average solute potential of cells at incipient plasmolysis:
- use of onion epidermis or other appropriate material
- calculate percentage plasmolysis
- determine the average solute potential from a graph of percentage plasmolysis against solute potential of the immersing solution; at 50% plasmolysis, the average pressure potential is zero

Examiner tip
In your revision, don't forget to include any practical work connected with water potential and solute potential.

Summary

- The basis of membrane structure is the phospholipid bilayer, with hydrophilic heads outermost and hydrophobic fatty acid tails innermost.
- Proteins span the bilayer (transmembrane proteins), or are embedded in or lie on the surface of the bilayer.
- Cholesterol is found in the hydrophobic centre of animal cell membranes.
- The fluid mosaic model suggests a fluid phospholipid bilayer with scattered protein molecules forming a mosaic pattern.
- Carbohydrates bind to produce glycoproteins and glycolipids on the outer surface of the cell-surface membrane where they form the glycocalyx and are involved in cell recognition and as cell receptors.

- Some proteins may act as enzymes.
- Lipid-soluble (non-polar) molecules and very small molecules (such as O_2 and CO_2) can move through the phospholipid bilayer.
- Transmembrane proteins may be involved in the movement of ions and water-soluble (polar) molecules.
- Ions may move by diffusion through the open pores of channel proteins, while water-soluble molecules (such as glucose) may move by facilitated diffusion through carrier proteins.
- Some water-soluble molecules may also be moved against the concentration gradient by active transport, via carrier proteins that use ATP to pump the molecules across.

- Water moleules can move through the phospholipid bilayer because they are so small, though more often they move through aquaporins.

- Osmosis is the diffusion of water from an area of high water potential to an area of lower water potential through a differentially (or partially) permeable membrane.

- Water potential has two components, solute potential and pressure potential.

- The presence of solutes in solution attracts water molecules and reduces the water potential (makes it more negative) as water is less free to move.

- Plant cells placed in water take in water and develop a pressure potential (turgor pressure) resisted by the cell wall. Animal cells burst when placed in water.

- Exocytosis is the secretion of large molecules (e.g. proteins) as a result of vesicles moving to, and fusing with, the cell-surface membrane.

- Endocytosis allows materials to be taken into the cell — large molecules into vesicles (pinocytosis) or larger materials (e.g. bacteria) into vacuoles (phagocytosis).

The cell cycle, mitosis and meiosis

The formation of new cells, for example in the development of a multicellular organism, involves the production of additional cell contents before a cell can divide. The pattern of events is called the **cell cycle**.

The cell cycle

Actively dividing eukaryotic cells pass through a series of stages known collectively as the cell cycle (Figure 45):

- **interphase** — two growth or **gap phases** (**G1** and **G2**) separated by a **synthesis (S) phase**
- **mitosis** — a nuclear division during which the chromosomal material is partitioned into daughter nuclei
- **cytokinesis** — the cell divides into two daughter cells

Examiner tip

The terms cell cycle (cell division) and mitosis are quite distinct and should not be confused. Mitosis is one form of nuclear division (the other is meiosis) and is the process by which the nucleus divides. The cell cycle (or cell-division cycle) is the series of events that take place leaving to its division and includes the phase of mitosis.

Knowledge check 47

When during the cell cycle does DNA replication take place?

Examiner tip

You must be able to distinguish between chromatid and chromosome. Once the centromere has split and the chromatids are separate, they are no longer chromatids but chromosomes, because each now has its own centromere.

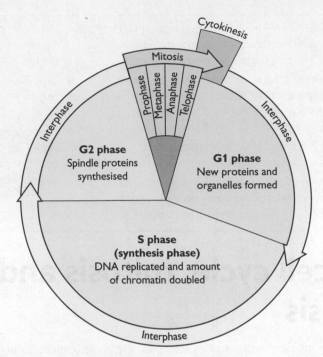

Figure 45 The cell cycle

Interphase

This is an intense period of metabolic activity as the cell synthesises new components such as organelles and membranes, and new proteins and DNA. This takes place in the following phases:

- G1 phase — synthesis of macromolecules, including proteins and nucleotides, occurs and the volume of the cytoplasm and the number of organelles increase rapidly.
- S phase — DNA synthesis occurs. Histones — proteins that bind to and support the DNA within the chromatids — are also produced. The DNA and chromatids formed are identical and remain attached until separated during mitosis (or meiosis).
- G2 phase — proteins such as tubulin are synthesised. Tubulin forms the microtubules of the spindle fibres.

Mitosis

During mitosis, different stages are recognised (see Figure 46).

Prophase

- The chromatin condenses to form the chromosomes
- The centrioles (in animal cells) move towards opposite poles
- The spindle begins to form
- As each chromosome continues to condense, two chromatids, joined at the centromere, become apparent

Metaphase

- The nuclear envelope breaks down
- Spindle formation is completed as microtubules extend, forming the fibres
- The microtubules of the spindle attach to the centromere of each chromosome
- The chromosomes (chromatid pairs) are moved by the microtubules onto the equator of the spindle

Anaphase

- The centromeres divide
- The spindle fibres pull the centromeres of sister chromatids apart
- The sister chromatids move towards opposite poles

Telophase

- Each chromatid is now a separate chromosome
- The two groups of chromosomes reach opposite poles of the the cell
- A new nuclear envelope forms around each group

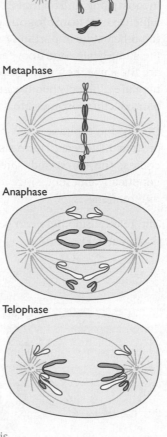

Figure 46 The stages of mitosis

Cytokinesis

At the end of mitosis, the cytoplasm is separated and the cell divides during cytokinesis to form two daughter cells. The process differs in animal and plant cells. In the animal cell, a **cleavage furrow** forms as protein microfilaments pull the cell surface membrane in along the equator; the furrow deepens and when the membranes fuse the cell is cleaved into two. In plant cells, the cell wall prevents cleavage. In the plant cell, the Golgi bodies (known as dictyosomes) produce vesicles that collect and fuse together to form an equatorial **cell plate**. The vesicles secrete the material of the middle lamella on each side of which a new cellulose cell wall is laid down.

Genes, chromosomes and ploidy

Specific lengths of DNA represent the **genes** (which code for the synthesis of proteins). The positions of genes on a chromosome are called **genetic loci** (singular: locus). During interphase, much of the DNA is unwound (**euchromatin**) in order to allow easy access to the code; some DNA remains condensed (the **heterochromatin**) because access to it is not required. At the onset of nuclear division (whether mitosis or meiosis)

> **Knowledge check 48**
>
> Describe one difference in nuclear division and one difference in cytokinesis between animal cells and plant cells.

all the chromatin becomes condensed (supercoiled); this increases its strength. The physical strength of the chromatids and chromosomes that form is important in preventing DNA breakage when they are pulled apart on the spindle apparatus.

In most plants and animals, the cells of the body each contain two sets of chromosomes, which exist in **homologous pairs**. Each member of a pair is similar in size and shape to the other. More importantly, they have the same genetic loci — they possess **alleles** of the same genes (one from each parent). If the alleles on the homologous chromosomes are the same then the individual is **homozygous** for that particular characteristic; if they are different then the individual is **heterozygous**. Cells containing homologous pairs of chromosomes are said to be **diploid** (represented by **2n**).

During the S phase, DNA replicates and each new DNA molecule associates with protein (histones) to form sister chromatids. Since DNA replication produces identical copies, the chromatids are genetically identical. Homologous chromosomes are genetically different, since at least some of the hundreds of genetic loci will possess different alleles.

The relationship between genes, alleles, chromatids and homologous chromosomes is shown in Figure 47.

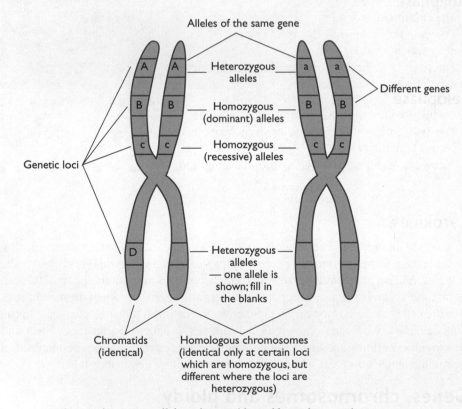

Figure 47 Genes, alleles, chromatids and homologous chromosomes

Knowledge check 49

Complete the alleles present at the D/d locus in Figure 47.

Knowledge check 50

If a cell has 15 chromosomes, is it likely to be diploid or haploid? Explain your answer.

A cell that contains only one of each type of chromosome is **haploid** (represented by **n**). Some simple organisms (e.g. mosses) contain cells with haploid nuclei but in higher forms it is only the gametes that are haploid.

Meiosis

Meiosis occurs only in diploid cells and produces haploid cells (e.g. gametes in animals). It involves the separation of homologous chromosomes during a first meiotic division (**meiosis I**) and the separation of chromatids during a second meiotic division (**meiosis II**). The apparatus for these divisions is the same as in mitosis, so the emphasis in Figure 48 is on points specific to meiosis.

Prophase I

- As chromosomes condense it becomes apparent that homologous chromosomes have paired and lie alongside each other; each pair is known as a bivalent
- The chromatids appear; the chromatids in a bivalent are entwined at points called chiasmata (singular: chiasma)
- The chromatids may break at chiasmata and rejoin with a different chromatid, resulting in crossing over or recombination

Metaphase I

- The bivalents move to the equator of the spindle
- Each chromosome of the pair becomes attached to a spindle fibre by its centromere

Anaphase I

- Pulling by the spindle fibres causes the whole chromosomes to move apart towards opposite poles
- The homologous chromosomes are separated; each chromosome still consists of two chromatids

Telophase I

- Chromosomes reach opposite poles of the cell.
- A nuclear membrane forms around each separate group of chromosomes; each nucleus contains the haploid number of chromosomes

Prophase I (late)

Metaphase I

Anaphase I

Telophase I

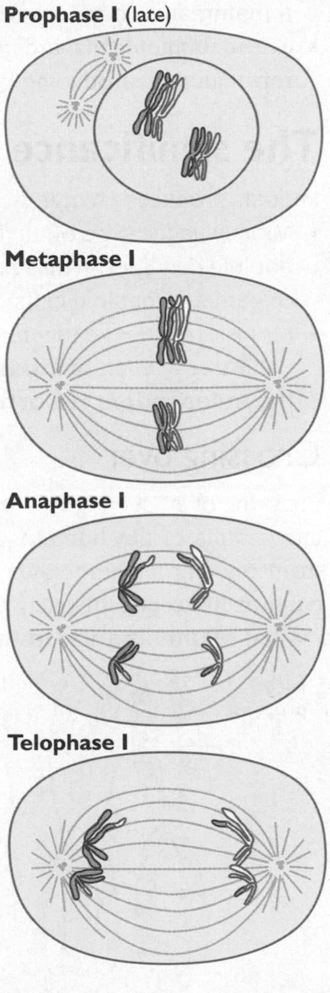

Figure 48 The stages of meiosis I

Examiner tip

Be aware that meiosis I is about the separation of the homologous chromosomes; meiosis II is about separation of the chromatids. So the chromosome number is halved after meiosis I, and the cells formed at this stage are haploid cells.

Knowledge check 51

In prophase I of meiosis, how many (a) chromatids and (b) chromosomes are there in one bivalent?

Examiner tip

Use the appearance and number of chromosomes at anaphase to identify whether a division is either mitotic or meiotic. If the chromosomes are double structures (two chromatids) it can only be anaphase I of meiosis. If they are single structures, it could be mitosis or anaphase II of meiosis. In that case look at how many there are. If the diploid number is moving to each pole, it must be mitosis; if the haploid number is moving to each pole, it must be meiosis II.

Cytokinesis after meiosis I produces two daughter cells. Within each, meiosis II follows:

- New spindles begin to form at right angles to the old spindle (**prophase II**).
- Chromosomes consisting of pairs of chromatids (now different because of crossing over) are arranged along the equator (**metaphase II**).
- Sister chromatids are split at the centromere and pulled to opposite poles (**anaphase II**).
- Each group of separated chromosomes becomes enclosed within a nuclear envelope (**telophase II**).

Cytokinesis follows. The overall result of meiosis is the production of four haploid daughter cells, each of which is genetically different from the others.

The significance of mitosis

Mitosis produces genetic constancy:

- The daughter cells possess the *same* chromosome number as each other and as the parent cell. Mitosis can occur in either diploid cells (e.g. during the development of a mammal) or haploid cells (e.g. in the growth of mosses).
- The daughter cells are *genetically identical*. Mitosis has a key role in asexual reproduction, producing genetically identical individuals (**clones**).

Examiner tip

When you are talking about mitosis or clones, you should always say 'genetically identical cells', not just 'identical cells'.

The significance of meiosis

Meiosis produces change:

- Meiosis is the type of nuclear division that transforms the diploid condition to the haploid condition. This is vital in life cycles where **fertilisation** involves the fusion of gametes (haploid cells) to form the zygote (a diploid cell).
- Meiosis produces daughter cells which are *genetically different*. This genetic variation occurs as a result of **crossing over** of chromatid pieces (during prophase I) and of the **independent assortment of bivalents** (during metaphase I).

Crossing over

Crossing over (see Figure 49) occurs as a result of chiasmata formation between the chromatids of the homologous pairs during late prophase I. A piece of chromatid from one chromosome swaps places with a piece of chromatid of the homologous partner. It results in each chromosome having a different combination of alleles (called **recombinants**) from that which occurred originally.

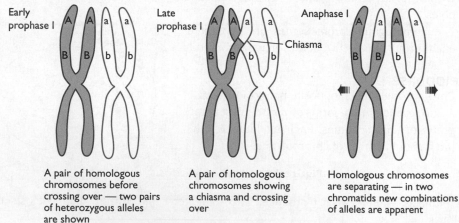

Figure 49 Crossing over and genetic variation

Knowledge check 52

After a single cross-over, how many chromatids in a bivalent have a new combination of alleles?

Independent assortment

During metaphase I, bivalents are arranged at *random* on the equator of the spindle. This means that the orientation of any one homologous pair is not dependent on the orientation of any other pair. When the homologous chromosomes are pulled apart at anaphase I, a chromosome of one pair is equally likely to be separated along with either member of any other homologous pair.

CCEA AS Biology

Independent assortment is illustrated in Figure 50.

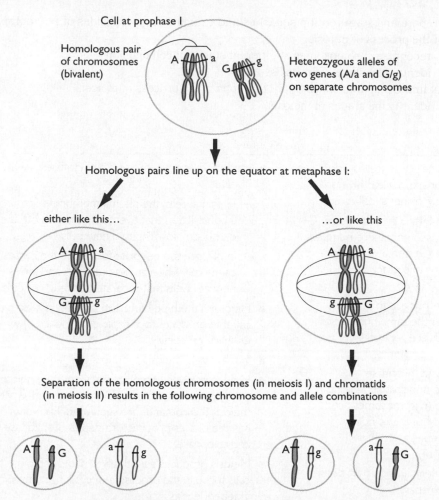

Figure 50 Independent assortment and genetic variation

Mitosis and meiosis are compared in Table 13.

Knowledge check 53

If diploid cells, $2n = 6$, divide by meiosis, how many different combinations of chromosomes would it be possible to find among the haploid cells produced?

Table 13 Comparison between mitosis and meiosis

Mitosis	Meiosis
One division, producing two daughter cells	Two divisions, producing four daughter cells
Parent cell may be either diploid or haploid; daughter cells have the same chromosome number as the parent cell	Parent cell is always diploid; daughter cells are haploid
Homologous chromosomes (if the parent cell is diploid) do not associate during prophase	Homologous chromosomes pair, forming bivalents during prophase I
No chiasmata formation	Chiasmata form between the chromatids of the homologous chromosomes during prophase I
Daughter cells are genetically identical	Daughter cells are genetically different

Practical work

Prepare and stain root tip squashes and examine prepared slides or photographs of the process of mitosis:
- recognise chromosomes at different stages of cell division
- identify the stages of mitosis

Examine prepared slides or photographs of the process of meiosis:
- identify the stages of meiosis

Summary

- Eukaryotic cells exhibit a cell cycle (cell-division cycle) consisting of interphase, nuclear division (mitosis or meiosis) and cytokinesis (cell division).

- Interphase is sub-divided into: a growth phase (G1) of biosynthesis and increase in organelle numbers; a DNA replication phase (S); and a second growth phase (G2), when proteins necessary for nuclear division are produced.

- Mitosis is a division of the nucleus to produce two daughter nuclei, with the same number of chromosomes, and which are genetically identical.

- Mitosis involves four phases: prophase (chromosomes condense and spindle assembly commences); metaphase (chromosomes are assembled on the equator of the spindle); anaphase (chromatids are separated); and telophase (new nuclei form).

- Mitosis is the type of nuclear division that occurs during growth and body repair.

- Nuclear division is followed by cytokinesis, which involves:
  - in animal cells, the plasma membrane forming a constriction that eventually 'pinches off' the cytoplasm, forming two new cells
  - in plant cells, a cell plate forming in the centre of the cell, which grows outwards and forms two new cell walls that separate the daughter cells

- Meiosis is the type of nuclear division in a diploid cell that produces four haploid cells, each of which will vary genetically.

- In mammals, meiosis produces the gametes.

- Meiosis involves two nuclear divisions: in meiosis I homologous chromosomes are separated, while in meiosis II chromatids are separated. Each division has the phases prophase, metaphase, anaphase and telophase.

- Meiosis produces genetically variable haploid cells through the processes of crossing over and independent assortment.

Tissues and organs

Animals and plants are multicellular — they are made up of large numbers of cells. Cells become specialised according to their function. **Tissues** are made up of many cells that perform one or several functions. Often the cells are of the same type. For example, epithelia are sheets of cells that line organs and separate internal tissues from air, blood, food and waste travelling through tubes in the body. In plants, the epidermis secretes a waxy cuticle to protect the plant from desiccation. **Organs** are structures made of several tissues that work together to carry out a number of functions. The **leaf** contains epidermis for protection, mesophyll for photosynthesis and gaseous exchange, xylem for transport of water and phloem for transport of sucrose. The **ileum** is the organ, in the small intestine, that is concerned with the final stages of digestion, the absorption of the products of digestion into blood vessels for transport to other parts of the body, and the movement of undigested material along to the large intestine. Many body processes are performed by groups of organs working together — **organ systems**. For example, in the digestive system of a mammal, the mouth, oesophagus, stomach, small and large intestines, liver, gall bladder and pancreas work together to digest and absorb food and eliminate undigested material.

The ileum

The ileum is the region of the small intestine where digestion is completed and where most absorption of the products of digestion occurs. There is a vast surface area for digestion and absorption provided by: folds in the inner surface of the intestinal wall; projections called **villi** (singular: villus) that are present on the folded surface of the wall; and microscopic projections called **microvilli** on the cell-surface membranes of **columnar epithelial cells** that line the villi.

Structurally the ileum consists of tissues in distinct layers: **mucosa**; **muscularis mucosa**; **submucosa**; **muscularis externa** and **serosa** (outermost) (see Figure 51).

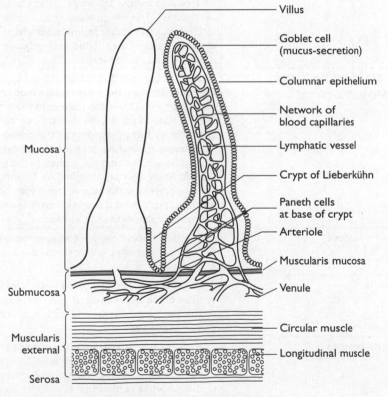

Figure 51 The structure of the ileum

The functions of the tissues are shown in Table 14.

Knowledge check 54

Name the tissue covering a leaf and the tissue covering the inner surface of the ileum.

Examiner tip

Students often confuse villi with microvilli. Villi are 1-mm projections of the wall of the mucosa and each contains thousands of cells. Microvilli are 0.6-μm projections of the cell-surface membrane of the epithelial cells lining the mucosa.

Examiner tip

Make sure that you distinguish between absorption (taking soluble molecules into the body) and assimilation (incorporating absorbed molecules into body tissues).

Table 14 The functions of tissues in the ileum

Tissue	Function
Columnar epithelium (within the mucosa)	This layer has column shaped cells and lines the intestine. On their free surfaces, the cells have microvilli, forming a brush border. Since digestive enzymes and carrier proteins are bound to the membrane of the microvilli, this provides a huge surface area for digestion and for the absorption of the products of digestion. Some substances are taken up partly by facilitated diffusion and partly by active transport; others are taken up by pinocytosis. There are numerous mitochondria to aid active transport. The cells of the epithelium are short-lived (see crypts of Lieberkühn).
Goblet cells (within the epithelium)	These cells secrete mucus. Mucus is slimy. It protects the epithelium from the action of digestive enzymes and lubricates the lining as solid material is pushed along.
Villi (within the mucosa)	These finger-like projections increase the surface area for the absorption of the products of digestion. The villi contain blood capillaries into which amino acids and monosaccharides are absorbed, and lacteals (blind-ending lymph vessels) into which fats are absorbed.
Crypts of Lieberkühn (within the mucosa)	These intestinal glands are found at the bases of the villi. The cells along the sides secrete mucus. The cells (stem cells) lining the bottom of the crypts are in a state of continuous division; new cells are continuously being pushed up by the division of cells deeper down. After a life of several days within the epithelium, the cells are pushed to the tips of the villi where they are sloughed off. Paneth cells are also present at the base of the crypts. Their function is to defend the actively dividing cells against microbes in the small intestine.
Muscularis mucosa	The muscle fibres contract to cause movement of the villi, so improving contact with the products of digestion.
Submucosa	The submucosa contains blood vessels including venules of the hepatic portal vein (carrying blood to the liver) and lymphatic vessels, supported by connective tissue.
Muscularis externa	The muscularis externa consists of circular muscle (innermost) and longitudinal muscle. Contraction of longitudinal muscle causes pendular movement of the gut while contraction of circular muscle may result in local constrictions, both of which churn the food. Coordinated contractions of the circular muscle push food along the gut by peristalsis.
Serosa	This outer layer of connective tissue serves to protect and support the gut.

Knowledge check 55

Explain why mucus is needed to protect the cells lining the ileum from protein-digesting enzymes.

Knowledge check 56

State one way in which the ileum is adapted to churn the food.

The leaf

The leaf has a large surface area which maximises the absorption of light for photosynthesis. It is thin, and so photosynthesising cells are not far from the leaf surfaces where light absorption and gaseous exchange occur.

Structurally, the leaf consists of epidermal layers either side of a middle layer of mesophyll and vascular tissues (see Figure 52).

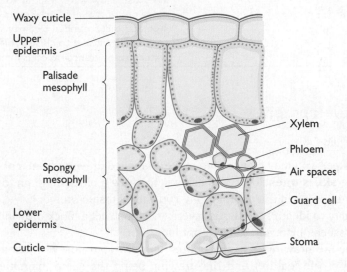

Figure 52 The structure of the leaf

The functions of the tissues are shown in Table 15.

Table 15 The functions of tissues in the leaf

Tissue	Function
Upper epidermis	The cells of the upper epidermis lack chloroplasts since their role is protective. They secrete a waxy cuticle that provides waterproofing and reduces water loss.
Palisade mesophyll	The palisade layer, in the upper half of the leaf, has layers of tightly packed cells, each with abundant chloroplasts. It is adapted for maximal light absorption. This is the main photosynthetic region of the leaf.
Spongy mesophyll	The mesophyll in the lower half of the leaf contains large air spaces. Gaseous exchange between these air spaces and the atmosphere can take place via numerous pores (stomata). Spongy mesophyll cells also contain chloroplasts and are photosynthetic.
Xylem vessels (within vascular bundles)	Xylem vessels supply the leaf with water and inorganic ions.
Phloem sieve tubes (within vascular bundles)	Phloem sieve tubes transport sucrose away from the leaf.

Knowledge check 57

Explain how the palisade mesophyll is adapted to carry out its function.

Knowledge check 58

What is the advantage to a plant of being able to control the opening and closing of stomata?

Table 15 The functions of tissues in the leaf (*continued*)

Lower epidermis	The cells lack chloroplasts. The cuticle secreted on the lower surface is thinner than that on the upper surface since it is not exposed directly to the sun.
Stomata	The lower epidermis contains numerous stomata which allow gaseous exchange. They also allow water vapour to diffuse easily out of the leaf. Each stoma (singular of stomata) is surrounded by a pair of guard cells which cause it to close at night and so water loss by transpiration is minimised.

Skills development

Drawing skills

In an AS paper, you may be asked to make a labelled drawing from a photograph. A **drawing skills question** could ask you to 'draw a block diagram to show the tissue layers shown in the photograph'. You will be tested on:

- your ability to identify the tissue layers and construct a block drawing showing all the tissues obvious in the photograph
- how true the drawing is to the photograph provided (and not just a textbook diagram of the feature) and the drawing being the same magnitude as the photograph (or having scale added if appropriate)
- the position and proportionality of the tissue layers
- the quality of the drawing so that clear, smooth and continuous lines are drawn

As an example, Figure 53 is a labelled drawing of a photograph of the midrib region of a privet leaf that shows the tissue layers.

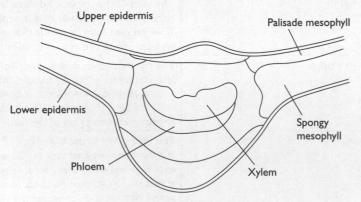

Figure 53 A block diagram of the midrib region of a privet leaf

Practical work

Examine stained sections of the ileum using the light microscope or photographs of the same:

- recognise the villi (and associated blood capillaries and lacteals), crypts of Lieberkühn (and Paneth cells), mucosa, columnar epithelium, goblet cells, muscularis mucosa, submucosa, muscularis externa and serosa

Examine sections of a mesophytic leaf using the light microscope or photographs of the same:

- recognise the epidermal layers, waxy cuticles, palisade mesophyll, chloroplasts, spongy mesophyll, vascular vessels with xylem and phloem, and guard cells and stomata

Make accurate drawings of sections of the ileum and the leaf to show the tissue layers:

- draw block diagrams of tissues within the ileum and the leaf

- An organ is a structure that consists of several different tissues, each performing different functions that contribute to the overall functioning of the organ.

- The ileum is the organ in mammals in which the final stages of digestion and most absorption take place.

- The absorptive surface is the columnar epithelium, with microvilli, on the villi of the mucosa layer.

- Monosaccharides and amino acids are absorbed into blood vessels but the products of fat digestion enter the lacteals (lymphatic vessels).

- Crypts of Lieberkühn possess stem cells, which produce new epithelial cells, and Paneth cells, which have an antimicrobial function.

- Contraction of the muscularis mucosa imparts a wafting action to the villi ensuring that they are in contact with freshly digested food.

- The submucosa contains blood and lymphatic vessels within connective tissue.

- The muscularis externa consists of circular and longitudinal muscles, which help to churn the food and move it along by peristalsis.

- The serosa covers the outside of the intestine and has a protective function.

- The leaf is the organ of photosynthesis in higher plants.

- The upper and lower epidermis are colourless and protect the leaf from damage and infection and, with the secretion of a waxy cuticle, from dehydration.

- Stomata are found mostly in the lower epidermis and open during the day to allow the diffusion of CO_2 into the leaf.

- The palisade mesophyll consists of columnar cells containing many chloroplasts and represents the main photosynthetic layer.

- The spongy mesophyll contains large air spaces which allow diffusion of gases through the leaf and contain chloroplasts for photosynthesis.

- The veins in the leaf contain the transport tissues xylem and phloem.

Summary

Questions & Answers

This section consists of two exemplar papers constructed in the same way as your AS Unit 1 examination papers. Following each question, there are answers provided by two students of differing ability.

Examiner's comments

Each question is followed by a brief analysis of what to look out for when answering the question (shown by the icon ⓔ). All student responses are then followed by examiner's comments. These are preceded by the icon ⓔ. They provide the correct answers and indicate where difficulties for the student occurred. Difficulties may include lack of detail, lack of clarity, misconceptions, irrelevance, poor reading of questions and mistaken meanings of examination terms. The comments suggest areas for improvement.

Using this section

You could simply read this section, but it would be more effective to:
- try the questions before looking at students' responses or the examiner's comments, allowing yourself 1 hour 30 minutes for each paper
- check your answers against the students' responses and the examiner's comments
- use the answers provided in the examiner's comments to mark your paper
- use the students' responses and the examiner's comments to check where your own performance might be improved

Tips for answering questions

Make sure that your answer is sufficiently detailed. The examiners give you guidance about how much you need to write:
- Use the mark allocation. Generally, the number of marks indicates the number of points that you should provide — for a question worth 4 marks you need to give more points than for one worth 2 marks.
- Use the recommended time allocation. You are advised to spend 20 minutes on Section B. Try to keep to this. It is possible to write a longer 'essay' but you may be providing more points than there are marks available.

Read the questions carefully. There are two aspects to this:
- Respond appropriately to the command terms used in each question, i.e. the verb the examiners use, e.g. 'describe' or 'explain' (see below).
- The stem of a question may provide information needed to answer the question. Think about how this information can help you to construct or focus on a relevant answer.

Command terms

You must understand the command terms used in questions. Appendix 1 of the specification and a guide in the biology microsite on www.ccea.org.uk explain these terms.

Exemplar paper 1

Section A

Question 1

Identify *four* distinct differences between mitosis and meiosis. (4 marks)

Total: 4 marks

ⓔ This question requires you to use your understanding of the two processes to identify differences — that is, what is evident in one process, but not in the other. In this question, it is important that the differences that you select are sufficiently distinct.

Student A

Mitosis consists of a single division, while there are two cell divisions in meiosis. ✓

Mitosis produces two cells, while meiosis produces four. ✗ **a**

In mitosis, the daughter cells are identical, while in meiosis the cells are genetically different. ✓ **b**

The daughter cells in mitosis are diploid, while the daughter cells in meiosis are haploid. ✗ **c**

ⓔ **2/4 marks awarded a** The first two answers, regarding number of divisions and the number of daughter cells produced, are not sufficiently distinct (two divisions will obviously produce twice the number of cells as a single division), so they only gain 1 mark. **b** Correct, and an important difference. **c** The fourth answer is incorrect. Meiosis always produces haploid cells, but mitosis produces diploid or haploid cells depending on the ploidy of the parent cell — it maintains the constancy of chromosome number.

Student B

Homologous chromosomes do not pair in mitosis, but do in meiosis. ✓

Chiasmata are not formed in mitosis, but are formed in meiosis. ✓

In mitosis, single chromosomes line up on the equator at metaphase; in meiosis, homologous pairs of chromosomes assemble on the equator at metaphase I. ✓

Mitosis produces genetically identical cells, while meiosis produces daughter cells that are genetically different. ✓ **a**

ⓔ **4/4 marks awarded a** All the answers are correct, scoring the maximum 4 marks. Note that these are not the only possible correct answers.

Question 2

The molecular diagram below illustrates a reversible reaction involving two amino acids.

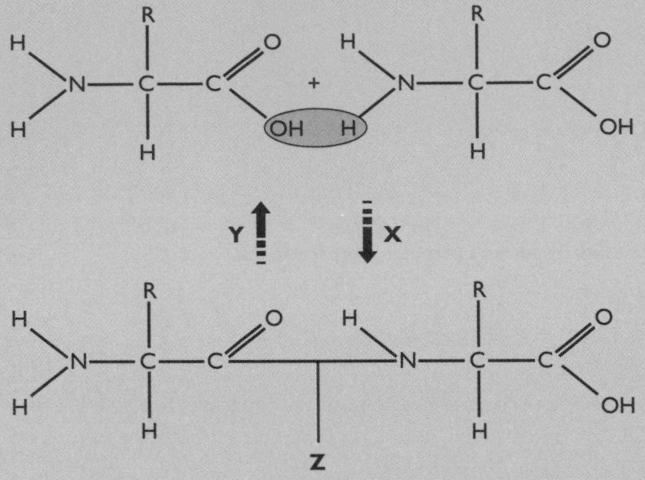

(a) (i) Name the type of reactions labelled X and Y.   (2 marks)
   (ii) Name the type of bond labelled Z.   (1 mark)
   (iii) Name the final product of reaction X.   (1 mark)

(b) Describe what is meant by the primary structure of a protein.   (1 mark)

Total: 5 marks

ℯ This question is, in fact, more straightforward than question 1. Part (a) tests recall (AO1) of types of reaction and bond formation between amino acids. In part (b) you need to define the primary structure of a protein.

Student A

(a) (i) X — condensation ✓
         Y — hydration ✗ a
   (ii) Amino bond ✗ b
   (iii) A diamine ✗ c
(b) A chain of amino acids ✗ d

ℯ **1/5 marks awarded a** Student A has confused the word hydration with hydrolysis. Hydration is the addition of water but this is breakdown by chemical reaction with water. **b** This student has simply not learnt or remembered that the bond joining two amino acids is a peptide bond. **c** Again, a lack of revision has meant forgetting that two amino acids bond to form a dipeptide. **d** This is not a sufficiently precise answer to earn a mark. 'The order or sequence of the amino acids in the chain' would be better wording.

Student B

(a) (i) X – condensation ✓
Y – hydrolysis ✓
(ii) Peptide bond ✓
(iii) A dipeptide ✓ **a**

(b) The sequence of bases ✗ and therefore the amino acid sequence. **b**

ⓔ **4/5 marks awarded a** All answers in part (a) are correct for 4 marks. **b** The sequence of amino acids is correct but not the sequence of bases leading to it. This is the genetic code — the order of base triplets that determines the primary structure of a protein. No mark can be awarded.

Question 3

The photograph below is an electron micrograph of part of a eukaryotic cell.

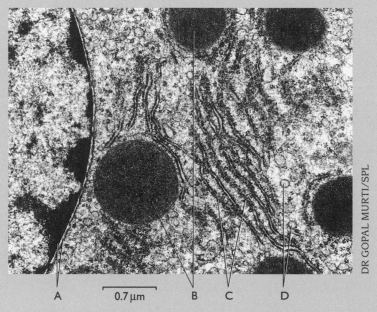

DR GOPAL MURTI/SPL

A   0.7 µm   B   C   D

(a) Identify the features labelled A to D. (4 marks)

(b) The photograph has a scale bar indicating 0.7 µm. Use this to calculate the magnification of this electron micrograph. Show your calculations. (3 marks)

Total: 7 marks

ⓔ Quite distinct skills are required in this question. Electron micrographs are always different from each other and, in part (a), you are required to identify four features within the specific EM provided. In part (b) you have to calculate the magnification of the EM, a skill that you should have previously practised.

Student A

(a) A — nuclear membrane ✗ **a**
   B — lysosomes ✗ **b**
   C — rough ER ✓ **c**
   D — vesicles ✓ **d**
(b) Length of scale bar = 1.4 cm long ✓ × 1000 = 1 400 μm ✗. Magnification = 1 400 × 0.7 = ×980 ✗ **e**

ⓔ **3/7 marks awarded a** This is the nuclear envelope or double membrane, so saying 'membrane' is not sufficiently accurate. **b** The answer to B is incorrect. The internal cristae are not so obvious in this micrograph (though visible in places), but the features are clearly covered by an envelope, so B are mitochondria. **c** Notice that ER is an accepted abbreviation for endoplasmic reticulum. **d** Correct. **e** Student A has measured the length of the scale bar correctly. However, measuring in centimetres has led to an incorrect conversion to micrometres. Further, if the measurement had been divided by 0.7 (the true length of the scale bar) instead of multiplying by 0.7, then another mark would have been scored. So, while the answer is wrong, 1 mark is scored because the 'working' clearly shows one correct operation.

Student B

(a) A — nuclear membranes ✓
   B — mitochondria ✓
   C — rough endoplasmic reticulum ✓
   D — ribosomes ✗ **a**
(b) The scale bar is 14 mm long ✓ which is 14 000 μm ✓, so magnification is 14 000 ÷ 0.7 = 20 000 times ✓ **b**

ⓔ **6/7 marks awarded a** The answer to D is incorrect. Ribosomes are solid structures and also smaller, as is apparent on the rough endoplasmic reticulum where the ribosomes are attached to sheets of membrane. The other answers are correct, so this scores 3 marks. Notice that the answer to A states the plural 'membranes'. **b** All stages in the calculation (measurement of scale bar, unit conversion and determination of magnification) are correct and clearly shown. Showing each stage is important because if a slip is made at any stage, marks can still be awarded for the correct procedure. This gains all 3 marks.

Question 4

The enzyme lactase catalyses the hydrolysis of lactose into galactose and glucose.

(a) Explain why lactase acts only on lactose and not on other disaccharides. (1 mark)

The graph below shows the effect of varying pH on lactase activity when in solution (○) and when immobilised (○).

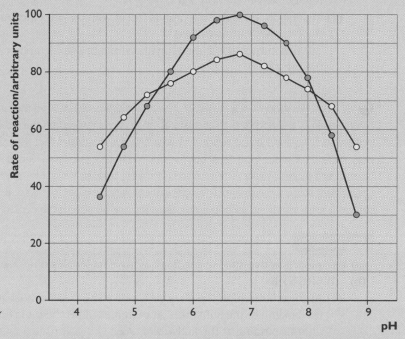

(b) Both in solution and when immobilised, lactase activity was maximal at a particular pH.
   (i) **Using the information in the graph, determine the optimal pH for lactase.** (1 mark)
   (ii) **Explain why enzymes exhibit an optimal pH.** (1 mark)

(c) (i) **Describe two differences in the activity of lactase in solution and when immobilised, as shown in the graph.** (2 marks)
   (ii) **Explain the differences you described in your answer to (c) (i).** (2 marks)

Total: 7 marks

ⓔ This question requires you to apply your understanding of enzyme action (AO2). You are not expected to have prior knowledge of the enzyme specified, lactase. Part (a) asks you to explain specificity. Part (b) (i) requires you to read accurately, from the graph, the optimal pH for lactase and explain it in (b) (ii). The activity of the enzyme, free in solution and immobilised, is then compared: part (c) (i) asks you to describe differences — to turn the differences shown in the curves into words — while (c) (ii) asks for explanations — reasons for the differences.

Student A

(a) The enzyme lactase has an active site with the same shape of lactose. ✗ **a**
(b) **(i)** pH 6.8 ✓ **b**
    (ii) It is the point at which there are most successful collisions. ✗ **c**
(c) **(i)** The enzyme in solution has a higher maximum rate of reaction than the immobilised enzyme. ✓
       The immobilised enzyme starts off and finishes the experiment with a higher rate of reaction. ✗ **d**
    (ii) In solution, the substrate bonds freely with the enzyme, but does not when the enzyme is immobilised. ✓
       When immobilised, the enzymes are more stable and are less affected by the pH. ✗ **e**

ℯ **3/7 marks awarded** **a** Incorrect. The active site does not have the *same* shape — it is *complementary* in shape to the substrate. **b** Value correctly read off the *x*-axis. **c** This is simply irrelevant. Temperature and concentration are factors that can affect the rate of collisions between enzyme and substrate molecules, but not pH. No mark can be awarded. **d** The first answer is correct and scores 1 mark. The second is incorrect because it assumes a time element, which is not evident in the experiment. The independent variable is pH, not time. **e** The first answer is sufficient for a mark. The second is not, since there is no attempt to *explain* the increase in stability.

Student B

(a) Because its active site is specific to lactose molecules only. ✗ **a**
(b) **(i)** pH 6.6 ✗ **b**
    (ii) At the optimum pH the enzyme's active site is at its most complementary for the binding of the substrate. At extremes of pH the ionic bonds are affected, altering binding at the active site. ✓ **c**
(c) **(i)** The immobilised enzyme has a lower rate of reaction at the optimum pH. ✓
       The immobilised enzyme is more active than the enzyme in solution at the extremes of pH. ✓ **d**
    (ii) Immobilised enzymes are physically bound within a substance (e.g. alginate) so the substrate cannot move as freely to the enzyme. ✓
       Immobilised enzymes are more stable because they are entrapped within a support material. ✓ **e**

ℯ **5/7 marks awarded** **a** This does not *explain* the specificity — for example, there is no mention of the lactase active site being complementary in shape to lactose. This fails to score. **b** Incorrect. Always try to make time to check through numerical work. This is obviously a slip — nevertheless, no mark can be awarded. **c** This is an excellent answer and scores the mark. **d** Both answers are correct, for 2 marks. **e** These are correct, well-phrased answers that earn both marks.

Question 5

An experiment was undertaken to determine the water potential of potato tuber tissue. The procedure was as follows:

(1) Obtain samples of tissue of approximately equal size
(2) Cut tissue samples into slices
(3) Surface-dry slices using filter paper
(4) Weigh tissue sample slices
(5) Add to one of a series of sucrose solutions of known solute potential
(6) Leave for 24 hours, after which surface-dry slices again and reweigh
(7) The change in mass is expressed as a percentage of the initial mass

(a) (i)   **Explain how equal-sized portions of tissue may be obtained.**
    (ii) **Explain why the tissue sample is cut into slices.**
    (iii) **Explain why the slices of tissue are surface-dried.**
    (iv) **Explain why the change in mass is expressed as a percentage.**   (4 marks)

The results of the experiment are shown in the graph below.

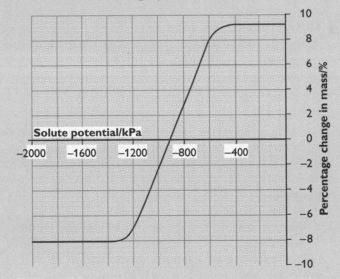

(b) **With reference to water potential, explain the change in mass that occurred when the slice of potato tissue was immersed in a sucrose solution of solute potential −600 kPa.**   (2 marks)

(c) **Using the information in the graph, determine the water potential of the potato tissue. Explain your reasoning.**   (2 marks)

(d) **In an evaluation of the experiment the importance of a 'standardised drying technique' was emphasised. Describe what is meant by a standardised drying technique, and explain its importance to the accuracy of the result.**   (2 marks)

Total: 10 marks

This question involves an investigation that you might have done in class — determining the water potential of potato tuber tissue. In part (a), and further in part (d), you are required to evaluate, and do so precisely, aspects of the procedure (AO3). In answering parts (b) and (c) you need to take time to study the graph of results — read the axes carefully and do not be put off by the negative scale. When you understand the graph, you are ready to explain the osmotic changes in (b) and then explain the determination of water potential in (c).

Student A

(a) **(i)** By using a cork borer ✗
   (ii) To increase the surface area for exchange ✓
   (iii) To remove any water from the surface that may affect the results ✓
   (iv) To make it easier to see the difference ✗ **a**

(b) Water moves from an area of high water potential to an area of low water potential ✓ and so moves out ✗ of the potato. **b**

(c) −850 kPa. ✗ The pressure potential is zero, so the water potential is equal to the solute potential. ✗ **c**

(d) The same pressure is applied to the filter paper when drying the potato discs, ✓ so that the results are reliable ✗. **d**

e **4/10 marks awarded** **a** The use of a cork borer alone is not sufficient because the cylinders have to be cut to the same length. The second and third answers, though correct, might have been more fully explained (see Student B's responses). The fourth answer is incorrect. 2 marks are scored. **b** Movement of water from high to low water potential is correct, for 1 mark. However, water does *not* move out of the potato tissue, since at −600 kPa there in an increase in the mass of the potato. **c** Student A has not accurately read the *x*-axis scale and needs to check numerical work. The reasoning given is not that for determining the water potential, but for determining the solute potential of, for example, epidermal tissue. Student A has confused the two experiments and fails to score. **d** The description of the standardised drying technique is correct, for 1 mark. However, its use has nothing to do with reliability, which is often confused with accuracy.

Student B

(a) **(i)** Use a cork borer of the same diameter and cut the cylinders to equal lengths ✓
   (ii) To provide a greater surface area over which osmosis can take place ✓
   (iii) To remove excess surface water that is not within the potato tissue ✓
   (iv) To allow changes in mass to be directly compared, since the tissue samples would not be the same mass to start with ✓ **a**

(b) With a solution of −600 kPa, the potato gains mass and so water must have entered it, ✓ which means that the potato tissue had a lower water potential ✓. **b**

(c) 900 kPa. ✗ At this point there is no percentage change in mass, which means that the water potential in the tissue and the sucrose solution is equal, ✓ so there is no net movement of water. **c**

(d) The same pressure has to be applied to the filter paper when drying before both initial and final weighings. ✓ If not sufficiently dried before the final weighing, then the weight loss would be less than it should have been. ✓ **d**

Question 6

(a) The active uptake of solutes by cells involves membrane carrier molecules. The carrier combines with the solute and then, utilising the energy of ATP, transfers it to the inner side of the membrane and releases it. The mechanism is represented in the diagram below.

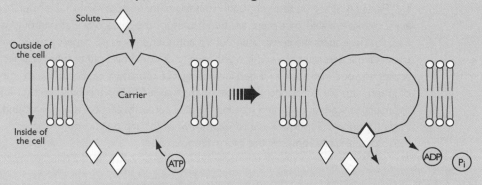

(i)   What type of molecule is the carrier? (1 mark)

(ii) For any particular solute that is absorbed actively there is a specific membrane carrier. Explain this specificity. (2 marks)

(iii) Explain how water passes through the membrane. (2 marks)

(b) The uptake of potassium ions by plant tissue placed in potassium chloride solution of different initial concentrations and at two different temperatures was investigated. The results of the experiment are shown in the table below.

Initial concentration of potassium chloride solution/mM	Uptake of potassium ions at 4°C/arbitrary units h⁻¹	Uptake of potassium ions at 18°C/arbitrary units h⁻¹
0	0	0
5	14	30
10	18	38
20	22	48
40	23	50

(i)   Plot the above data, using the most appropriate graphical technique. (4 marks)

(ii) The plant tissue has an internal potassium ion concentration of 50 mM. Explain why the potassium uptake must involve active transport. (1 mark)

(iii) Explain the effect of temperature on the rate of potassium ion uptake. (2 marks)

(iv) Active transport involves membrane carrier molecules with which the ions combine before being transferred to the inner side of the membrane. Use this information to suggest why at 18°C:

- **increasing the concentration of potassium ions from 0 mM to 20 mM greatly increases the rate of uptake**
- **increasing the concentration of potassium ions from 20 mM to 40 mM does not appreciably increase the rate of uptake** (2 marks)

(v) Rubidium ions have similar properties to potassium ions and, when present in the external solution, reduce the rate of potassium ion uptake. Suggest a reason for this observation. (1 mark)

Total: 15 marks

ⓔ Parts (a) (i) and (ii) test your understanding of membrane carriers. Be careful in (a) (iii), there are 2 marks available since there are two routes for the passage of water through a membrane. Part (b) (i) requires the construction of a graph. Generally in AS papers you are required to undertake a skills activity — where you have to *do* something rather than recall facts or work something out. Marks are awarded for writing an explanatory caption, choosing the correct type of graph with the independent variable on the *x*-axis, labelling the axes correctly and choosing an appropriate scale for each, and plotting the data correctly, appropriately joined and with a key. Parts (b) (ii) and (iii) require you to 'explain', while (iv) and (v) ask you to 'suggest' — provide a reasonable explanation using the information supplied.

Student A

(a) (i) Protein ✓ **a**
(ii) Fat-soluble molecules go through the phospholipid bilayer, and water-soluble molecules go through the hydrophilic channels. ✗ **b**
(iii) Through the hydrophilic channels. ✗ **c**

(b) (i)

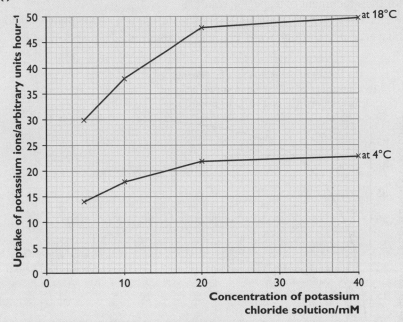

(ii) There is a greater concentration of potassium chloride inside than there is outside, so it can't move by diffusion. ✓ **e**
(iii) As temperature increases, the rate of ion uptake increases since the ions have more kinetic energy. ✗ **f**
(iv) From 0mM to 20mM: more potassium ions are available for attachment to the carriers. ✓
From 20 to 40mM: there are a limited number of carrier proteins to transport the potassium ions. ✓ **g**
(v) They inhibit the carrier proteins by taking the place of K⁺ ions. ✓ **h**

🅔 **7/15 marks awarded a** This is correct, for 1 mark. **b** Student A has not read the question carefully enough. The question requires an explanation of the specificity of membrane carriers. Student A fails to score. **c** This is not sufficiently precise — water molecules pass through specific water channel proteins (aquaporins) *and* are small enough to pass through the phospholipid bilayer. No marks scored. **d** There is no caption to explain the contents of the graph; ✗ a line graph is chosen and the concentration of potassium chloride solution is the independent variable; ✓ both axes have labels with units of measurement and appropriately scaled; ✓ the 0,0 points are not plotted and so the initial part of the graph is missing (though points are appropriately joined with short, straight lines and the lines for 4°C and 18°C are identified); ✗ Student A scores 2 of the 4 marks available. **e** This is correct, for 1 mark. **f** In part (b) (ii) it was established that ion uptake does not occur by diffusion. The answer should relate to the availability of ATP for the operation of the membrane carriers (see Student B's response). No marks can be awarded. **g** The answers to both parts of the graph are correct, for 2 marks. **h** This is correct, for 1 mark.

Student B

(a) **(i)** Protein ✓ **a**

(ii) Each carrier protein has a receptor site ✓ that has a complementary shape ✓ for the attachment of a specific solute. **b**

(iii) Water molecules are sufficiently small to diffuse across the phospholipid bilayers ✓ and through water channel proteins called aquaporins ✓. **c**

(b) **(i)**

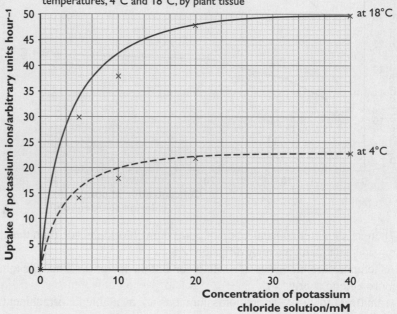

The uptake of potassium ions in different concentrations of KCl solution at two different temperatures, 4°C and 18°C, by plant tissue

(ii) There is a greater concentration of potassium chloride inside than outside, so it can't move in by diffusion. ✓ **e**

(iii) At higher temperature, the rate of respiration is greater ✓, so more ATP is available for the action of the carriers in active transport. ✓ **f**

(iv) From 0 mM to 20 mM: there are more ions available for transport. ✗ From 20 to 40 mM: the carrier proteins are functioning at their maximum rate. ✓ **g**

(v) Rubidium ions inhibit respiration. ✗ **h**

ⓔ 12/15 marks awarded **a** This is correct, for 1 mark. **b** This scores both marks. **c** Both routes are correct, for 2 marks. **d** An appropriate caption noting K^+ uptake, potassium chloride concentration and temperature is included; ✓ a line graph is drawn with the concentration of potassium chloride solution as the independent variable; ✓ both axes have labels with units of measurement and appropriately scaled; ✓ the points are accurately plotted but joined by curved lines, which are not best-fit. ✗ Student B scores 3 marks. **e** This is correct, for 1 mark. **f** Student

B has correctly identified that active transport requires ATP, and that the rate of respiration is dependent on the temperature. This scores both marks. **g** The answer to the first part should have specified the frequency of attachment of the ions to the carrier proteins. The answer to the second part is correct and earns 1 mark. **h** This would reduce the rate of K$^+$ ion uptake, but the answer does not use the information given in the question — that rubidium ions have similar properties to potassium ions. This answer fails to score.

Question 7

(a) **The polymerase chain reaction (PCR) enables many copies of DNA to be made from a small sample. The diagram below summarises the procedure.**

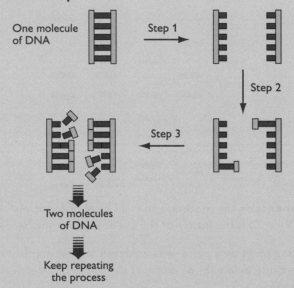

(i) **Explain what is happening at each of the following steps:**
   – **Step 1**
   – **Step 2**
   – **Step 3** (3 marks)
(ii) **At the end of the first cycle, there are two molecules of DNA. How many molecules will there be at the end of five cycles?** (1 mark)

(b) **DNA fingerprinting (profiling) is based on the genetic uniqueness of each individual (identical twins excepted). Particular enzymes are used to cut human DNA at specific sites to produce fragments of different length. The DNA fragments are separated by gel electrophoresis (which distinguishes the fragments on the basis of size) to produce a series of bands. Each person's DNA produces a unique set of bands.**
   (i) **Name the type of enzyme used to cut DNA, and explain how the site is recognised by the enzyme.** (2 marks)
   (ii) **Suggest why this type of enzyme cuts the DNA to produce fragments of different lengths.** (1 mark)

The results of DNA fingerprinting can provide strong evidence in cases of disputed parenthood. The diagram below represents DNA fingerprints of a mother (M) and her child (C), and those of three men (X, Y and Z).

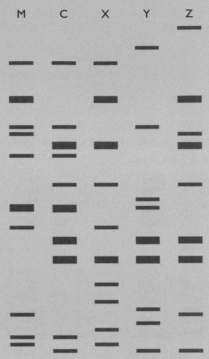

(iii) How many DNA fragments do the mother and child have in common? (1 mark)

(iv) Which individual (X, Y or Z) is the father of the child? Explain your answer. (2 marks)

(c) A DNA fragment, consisting of 24 base pairs, was analysed for the number of different bases on each strand. The table below shows some of the results. Determine the missing values and complete the table.

	A	G	T	C
Strand 1	7	8		
Strand 2	4			

(2 marks)

Total: 12 marks

In part (a) (i), you must use your understanding of the PCR to explain steps in the procedure and not just describe them. An arithmetic calculation is required in (a) (ii). All exam papers will test numeracy so you should have practised a variety of calculations. In parts (b) (i) and (ii), you are required to show recall of how DNA fragments are cut during DNA fingerprinting; while, in (b) (iii) and (iv), you will need to interpret fingerprints in a paternity case. Part (c) tests your understanding of base pairs — make sure that you use all the information provided.

Student A

(a) **(i)** Step 1: the strands are separated. ✗

Step 2: DNA primers are added to ensure that the two strands don't immediately rejoin. ✓

Step 3: more nucleotides are added and attach to the DNA strands under the control of DNA polymerase. ✓ **a**

(ii) 64 ✗ **b**

(b) **(i)** Restriction endonuclease ✓ recognises the highly repetitive 4-base sequences ✗ in the non-coding sections of DNA. **c**

(ii) The length of the fragments depends on the number of repeat sequences. ✗ **d**

(iii) 5 ✓ **e**

(iv) Z ✓, since only Z produces those fragments not supplied by the mother ✓. **f**

(c) Strand 1: T = 7, C = 8 ✗

Strand 2: G = 5, T = 4, C = 5 ✗ **g**

ⓔ **6/12 marks awarded** **a** The answer to step 1 does not provide sufficient detail, i.e. that heating to 95°C breaks the hydrogen bonds between the two strands. The answers to steps 2 and 3 are correct. Student A scores 2 marks. **b** This is incorrect — Student A has multiplied by 2 one time too many. **c** The enzyme name is correct, but Student A does not understand about the recognition sites. There is confusion with the microsatellite repeat sequences (MRSs) used in DNA profiling. Student A scores 1 mark for restriction endonuclease. **d** The confusion with MRSs is continued. Student A fails to score. **e** This is correct, for 1 mark. **f** Individual Z is correctly identified and the explanation is excellent. Student A scores both marks. **g** Student A has equal numbers of A and T bases and of G and C within each strand, rather than *between* the strands (see the answers provided by Student B). Student A fails to score.

Student B

(a) **(i)** Step 1: the DNA is heated to 95°C to break the hydrogen bonds. ✓

Step 2: DNA primers anneal to the end of each strand to initiate replication. ✓

Step 3: the mixture is heated again and a heat-sensitive DNA polymerase catalyses the addition of complementary nucleotides. ✓ **a**

(ii) 32 ✓ **b**

(b) **(i)** Restriction endonuclease ✓ recognises a specific sequence of bases ✓. **c**

(ii) The correct base sequence fits into the active site of the enzyme. ✗ **d**

(iii) 6 ✗ **e**

(iv) Z ✓, because this individual possesses the most bands in common with the child ✗. **f**

(c) Strand 1: T = 4, C = 5 ✓

Strand 2: G = 5, T = 7, C = 8 ✓ **g**

ⓔ **9/12 marks awarded** **a** All the steps are described fully. Student B scores all 3 marks. **b** This is correct, for 1 mark. **c** The enzyme and its recognition site are identified correctly, for 2 marks. **d** This does not explain the different number of fragment lengths, i.e. that the specific base sequence occurs at irregular intervals along the DNA. No mark can be awarded. **e** This is incorrect

and seems careless. **f** Individual Z is identified correctly, for 1 mark. However, the reasoning is incorrect. It is not just a matter of the number of common bands. The father must provide those fragments (bands) not inherited from the mother. **g** This is correct. Student B understands base pairing between the two strands (A to T and C to G) and has taken into account a total of 24 bases in each strand (information supplied in the stem). Student B scores both marks.

ⓔ **Section A total for Student A: 26 marks out of 60. Section A total for Student B: 49 marks out of 60.**

Section B

Quality of written communication is awarded a maximum of 2 marks in this section.

Question 8

Give an account of the structure and function of the following polysaccharides:
- **starch**
- **glycogen**
- **cellulose** (13 marks)

Quality of written communication (2 marks)

Total: 15 marks

ⓔ In this question, worth 15 marks, you are to write in continuous prose because 2 marks are awarded for quality of written communication (QWC). Remember to write about both structure and function of the three polysaccharides. Taking some time to devise a *plan* for your 'account' will benefit you, particularly in being able to sequence your ideas and emphasise the links between structure and function, which is how QWC will be assessed.

Student A

Starch is usually found in plants. It is an energy store in plants ✓ and its glucose isomers are composed from α-glucose ✓. It is a branched structure and has no hydrogen bonds present. Glycosidic bonds are present. **a**

Glycogen is found in the liver and muscles ✓ of animals. It is the energy store ✓ and its glucose isomers are composed of α-glucose and β-glucose. It is a branched structure and also has glycosidic bonds present. **b**

Cellulose is found in the cell walls in plants. ✓ It has many functions, which include a food source, a structural component of the cell wall and for tensile strength. It is composed of β-glucose ✓ and glycosidic bonds are present. **c; QWC d**

(e) **7/15 marks awarded** **a** Two marking points are given. The other information is not sufficiently detailed — for example, starch cannot be described as branched when branching only occurs in its amylopectin component. **b** Two appropriate points are provided. It is wrong to say the glycogen is a polymer of α-glucose and β-glucose — it is a polymer of α-glucose. Detail is also lacking — branching should be explained as due to 1,6-glycosidic bonds to be worthy of a mark. **c** There are two points worthy of marks. Other phrases lack detail — for example, tensile strength is not explained and is not by itself sufficient to earn a mark. **d** The account has a reasonable structure but connections between the points are not sufficiently well established. 1 mark is awarded for quality of written communication.

Student B

Starch is the energy store in plants ✓ and is made up of amylose and amylopectin. ✓ Both are polymers of α-glucose. ✓ They are helical molecules and so compact ✓ while amylopectin is branched due to 1,6-glycosidic bonds ✓. **a**

Glycogen is the energy store in animals ✓ particularly in the liver and muscle tissue ✓. It is also a polymer of α-glucose ✓ and is similar to amylopectin in that it is branched due to the presence of 1,6-glycosidic bonds ✓. The many terminal ends mean that it can be rapidly hydrolysed ✓. **b**

Cellulose is the structural polysaccharide found in the plant cell wall. ✓ It is a polymer of β-glucose ✓ and so forms straight chains ✓. The cellulose molecules hydrogen bond together ✓ forming microfibrils ✓ of high tensile strength ✓. **c; QWC d**

(e) **15/15 marks awarded** **a** Five marking points are given. **b** Five appropriate points are provided. **c** Here, there are six points worthy of marks. However, Student B can only score a maximum of 3 marks because 10 marks have been awarded already. **d** The account is well-structured and the statements are well-linked throughout. 2 marks are awarded for quality of written communication.

(e) **Section B total for Student A: 7 marks out of 15. Section B total for Student B: 15 marks out of 15.**

(e) **Paper total for Student A: 33 marks out of 75, which equates to a grade E. There is evidence of a lack of preparation for the paper. Too often straightforward knowledge is absent (e.g. in question 2 on amino acid synthesis) or there is a failure to provide sufficient detail (as in question 4 on immobilised enzymes and question 8 on polysaccharide structure and function). Numeracy skills are a problem (questions 3 (b) and 7 (c)) while the ability to evaluate practical work proves difficult (question 5). Nevertheless, there is sufficient material presented to ensure that a pass grade is appropriate in that some questions are tackled reasonably well (questions 6 and 7).**

Paper total for Student B: 64 marks out of 75, which is a grade A performance. Student B demonstrates a greater breadth of knowledge and is able to provide detailed answers. Numeracy skills are well represented, while there is ample evidence of an ability to evaluate information and analyse data. Ideas are well expressed and good use has been made of appropriate biological terminology.

Exemplar paper 2

Section A

Question 1

Read through the following passage on the cell cycle, and write the most appropriate words in the blank spaces to complete the account.

Actively dividing eukaryotic cells go through a process called the cell cycle. During .... there are intense periods of growth within which there is a .... phase when **DNA** replication occurs. In the nuclear division, mitosis, four phases are recognised. In the first of these, the chromosomes shorten and thicken, and each is seen to consist of a pair of chromatids. In the next phase, known as .... , the chromosomes assemble across the equatorial plane. This is followed by a phase during which two nuclei form. .... follows nuclear division and involves the division of cytoplasm and the formation of two daughter cells. Two nuclear divisions occur during meiosis so that the chromosome number is ....

(4 marks)

Total: 4 marks

ⓔ In this question you have to complete a passage on the cell cycle. You should read the whole passage through before endeavouring to add words in the blank spaces. Notice that you will need to get all five words for the maximum 4 marks.

Student A

Interphase ✓; synthesis ✓; metaphase ✓; anaphase ✗; 23 ✗ **a**

ⓔ **2/4 marks awarded a** The first three responses are correct and earn 2 marks. Cytokinesis follows nuclear division, so anaphase is incorrect. Student A has not read the passage carefully enough. Meiosis produces haploid cells — 23 is correct only for human cells and so cannot be awarded a mark.

Student B

Interphase ✓; synthesis ✓; metaphase ✓; cytokinesis ✓; hapliod ✓ **a**

ⓔ **4/4 marks awarded a** All five answers are correct and earn the full 4 marks. Even though the spelling of haploid is incorrect it is not sufficiently poor as to prevent recognition.

Question 2

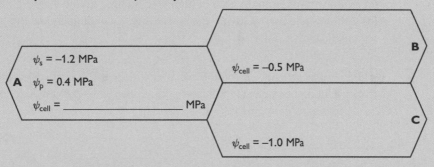

The diagram below represents three adjacent plant cells.

(a) Calculate the water potential of cell A. (1 mark)

(b) Show, by drawing arrows on the diagram, the direction of water movement between the three cells. (2 marks)

(c) With reference to water potential, explain why water moves in the direction that you indicated. (1 mark)

(d) Explain what would happen to the water potential of cell A if sugars were produced in the cell. (1 mark)

Total: 5 marks

ⓔ In part (a) you need to calculate the water potential of a cell and show understanding of water flow between regions of different water potential in part (b). In part (c) the water movement *must* be explained with reference to water potential — the examiners could not be more clear. The consequence of sugar production on water potential is tested in part (d).

Student A

(a) For cell A, $\Psi_{cell} = 0.8\,\text{MPa}$ ✗ **a**
(b) Arrows from A to C ✓, B to A ✓ and B to C **b**
(c) Water moves from high concentration to low concentration. ✗ **c**
(d) Ψ_{cell} would increase as the presence of more solutes means that Ψ_s would become higher. ✗ **d**

ⓔ **2/5 marks awarded a** This is incorrect since the negative sign has been omitted. **b** The arrows are all correct, for 2 marks. **c** This is incorrect, since the term water potential, requested in the question, is not used. Always take care when reading questions. The term concentration is too vague because it could refer to either water or solute. It is preferable to think about the amount of 'free' water, i.e. the water molecules that are not attracted to solute molecules. Student A fails to score. **d** Student A has forgotten that the addition of solutes decreases the solute potential and so consequently Ψ_{cell} also becomes lower. Student A fails to score.

Student B

(a) $\Psi_{cell} = -0.8\,\text{MPa}$ ✓ **a**

(b) Arrows from A to C ✓, B to A ✓ and B to C **b**

(c) Water moves from an area of high Ψ to an area of low Ψ (more negative). ✓ **c**

(d) Cell A would have a lower Ψ_{cell} as the sugar would decrease the Ψ_s of the cell (as $\Psi_{cell} = \Psi_s + \Psi_p$). ✓ **d**

🅔 **5/5 marks awarded a** This is correct, for 1 mark. **b** The arrow directions are all correct, for 2 marks. **c** Student B understands that −1 is lower than both −0.8 and −0.5, and earns the mark. **d** This full answer earns the mark.

Question 3

(a) Four test tubes each contained a solution of a single carbohydrate: fructose, glucose, sucrose or starch. The test tubes were labelled A to D and, in order to identify the carbohydrate present in each tube, a series of tests was carried out.

(1) Samples from all four tubes were tested with iodine solution. Tube B tested positive.

(2) Samples from the remaining three tubes were tested with clinistix. Tube A tested positive.

(3) Samples from the remaining two tubes were tested using Benedict's test. Tube D tested positive.

The remaining tube can be identified by elimination.

(i) Using the test results shown above, identify the carbohydrate in each of tubes A to D, and complete the table below. (3 marks)

Tube	Carbohydrate
A	
B	
C	
D	

(ii) Complete the table below to indicate a positive result for each test. (2 marks)

Test	Positive result
Iodine	
Clinistix	
Benedict's	

(b) Sugars, particularly sucrose, are added to soft drinks as sweeteners. However, not all sugars impart the same level of sweetness. Glucose has only 75% of the sweetness of sucrose but fructose is twice as sweet as glucose. Determine how much fructose must be added to replace 30 g of sucrose. Show your working. (2 marks)

Total: 7 marks

CCEA AS Biology

ⓔ In part (a) (i) you are presented with a problem-solving situation involving the identification of four carbohydrates (notice for 3 marks), while understanding of end-point colours for three tests is required in (b) (ii) (for 2 marks). In part (b) you are given a numeric problem to solve — if the solution does not come readily, you should return to this part later when your confidence has grown.

Student A

(a) (i) A — fructose ✗
B — starch ✓
C — glucose ✗
D — sucrose ✗ **a**
(ii) Iodine — blue–black ✓
Clinistix — purple ✓
Benedict's — orange–red ✓ **b**
(b) 75% of 30 g = 22.5 g ✗
22.5 ÷ 2 ✓ = 11.25 g **c**

ⓔ **4/7 marks awarded a** Only the iodine test for starch has been identified correctly. The tests for the sugars are not well understood. Clinistix is a specific test for glucose (test A), while sucrose is not a reducing sugar and, therefore, does not give a positive result with Benedict's solution (test D). Student A gains only 1 mark. **b** All three responses are correct, for 2 marks. **c** If glucose has 75% of the sweetness of sucrose, then more of it is required to give the same level of sweetness. So 40 g of glucose equates to 30 g of sucrose, which equates to 20 g (40 ÷ 2) of fructose, since fructose is twice as sweet as glucose. Student A has not got the first relationship, but understands to divide by 2 for the link between glucose and fructose and so earns 1 mark.

Student B

(a) (i) A — glucose ✓
B — starch ✓
C — sucrose ✓
D — fructose (✓) **a**
(ii) Iodine — blue–black ✓
Clinistix — colourless ✗
Benedict's — brick-red ✓ **b**
(b) sweetness of fructose = 150% (75% × 2) sweetness of sucrose ✓
so 30 g ÷ 150% = 20 g ✓ **c**

ⓔ **6/7 marks awarded a** All answers are correct, for 3 marks. Notice that since the first three answers are correct the fourth must be correct. **b** The end-point colour for the Clinistix test is purple, although a range of colours from purple to blue is acceptable. There is also an acceptable range of colours for a positive Benedict's test. Two correct responses gain 1 mark. **c** Student B has worked out the relationships well and seems at ease with numerical problems. Both marks are awarded.

Question 4

(a) **The diagram below shows the structure of a typical prokaryotic cell (a bacterium).**

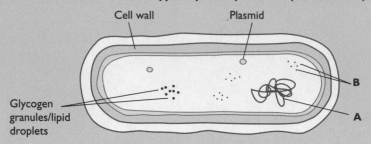

(i) **Identify the structures labelled A and B.** (2 marks)

(ii) **Suggest one function of each of the following structures found in the bacterial cell:**
- **glycogen granules**
- **cell wall** (2 marks)

(b) **Mitochondria are absent from prokaryotic cells but are present in eukaryotic cells. Describe the structure and function of mitochondria.** (2 marks)

(c) **Viruses occur in a variety of forms, including bacteriophages (phages) and the human immunodeficiency virus (HIV).**

(i) **List the molecules of which all viruses are composed.** (2 marks)

(ii) **Explain why viruses are not regarded as living cells.** (1 mark)

Total: 9 marks

Ⓔ Part (a) (i) requires you to 'identify' two structures of a bacterial cell and part (ii) to 'suggest' functions for two features. You should use understanding of animal and plant cells to help you. You are asked to 'recall' the structure and function of mitochondria in part (b). In part (c), you need to 'list' the chemical components of viruses in (i) and, while the answer to (ii) may be obvious, you need to provide a sufficiently detailed answer.

Student A

(a) **(i)** A — chromosome ✗
　　　　B — ribosomes ✓ **a**

(ii) Glycogen granules — to store food ✗
　　　　Cell wall — to provide support ✓ **b**

(b) Mitochondria have an envelope of two membranes, the inner being folded to form cristae. ✓ They are used to produce energy. ✗ **c**

(c) **(i)** Protein, ✓ DNA ✗ **d**

(ii) They need a host to do anything. ✗ **e**

Ⓔ **4/9 marks awarded a** The first answer is not correct since bacteria possess 'naked' chromosomes consisting of DNA but lacking the associated histones. The second is correct.
b Glycogen is a store of glucose (energy) — suggesting that it is a store of food is too vague. The cell wall does provide support and a mark is awarded. However, Student B provides a better

answer. **c** The structure is sufficiently well described. However, it is not precise enough to say that mitochondria produce energy. They produce ATP through aerobic respiration. Student A gains 1 mark. **d** All viruses contain protein, but not all contain DNA. Some, such as HIV, contain RNA. Student A earns 1 mark for protein. **e** This could be describing any parasite. Student A fails to score.

Student B

(a) (i) A — DNA ✓; B (blank) ✗ **a**
  (ii) Glycogen granules — store glucose for respiration ✓
     Cell wall — a structural role in preventing osmotic bursting of the cell ✓ **b**
(b) Mitochondria are surrounded by two membranes with the inner membrane folded to form cristae. ✓ They contain a matrix with small ribosomes and a circular DNA molecule. In aerobic respiration much of the cell's ATP is produced. ✓ **c**
(c) (i) Protein, ✓ nucleic acid ✓ **d**
  (ii) Viruses have no cellular structure or metabolic activity, and can only replicate using the metabolism of a host cell. ✓ **e**

ⓔ **8/9 marks awarded a** A is correct, for 1 mark. B can only really be ribosomes — they cannot, for example, be vesicles since a prokaryotic cell has no membrane-bound organelles. **b** These full answers earn both marks. **c** This excellent answer contains more than is required for the 2 marks. **d** Both answers are correct, for 2 marks. **e** This excellent answer earns the mark.

Question 5

The photograph below is a photomicrograph of a transverse section through part of the wall of the small intestine (ileum).

Draw a block diagram to show the tissue layers in the ileum, as shown in the photograph. Label the drawing to identify at least five structures.

(9 marks)

Total: 9 marks

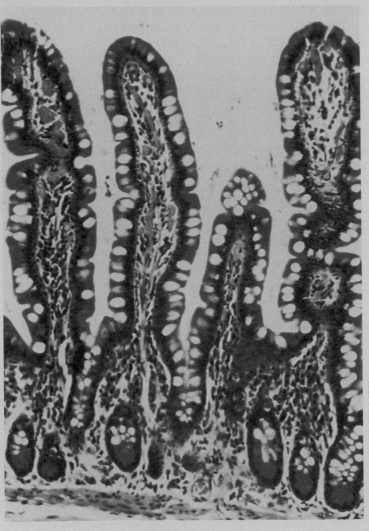

BIOPHOTO ASSOCIATES/SPL

This question involves *drawing* — the skills activity in this paper. You also have to identify five structures. Notice that the outer layers of the ileum are not included in the photomicrograph. There are 4 marks for drawing skills and 5 marks for identification. Drawing skills marks are awarded for drawing the obvious tissue layers, ensuring that your drawing is that of the photo supplied, that the proportionality of the drawing is accurate and that drawn lines are clear and not sketchy.

CCEA AS Biology

Student A

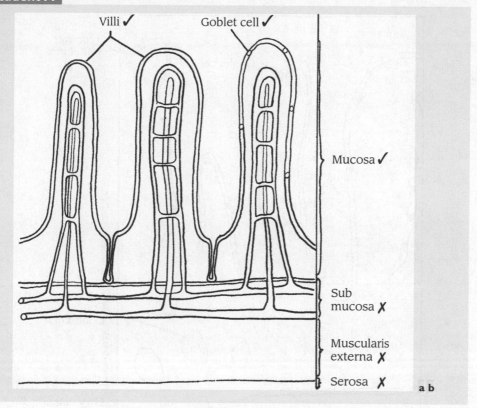

Villi ✓   Goblet cell ✓

Mucosa ✓

Sub
mucosa ✗

Muscularis
externa ✗

Serosa ✗

a b

ℯ **5/9 marks awarded** **a** This is a block diagram showing the tissue layers of those tissues obvious in the photograph. ✓ However, it is a well-learned textbook diagram, which does not accurately represent the photograph ✗ and lacks the proportionality of the features shown ✗. The lines drawn are smooth and continuous, not sketchy. ✓ Student A earns 2 marks out of 4 for drawing skills. **b** Student A has three features correct, for 3 marks. The layers submucosa, muscularis externa and serosa are not included in the photograph and so cannot be awarded marks.

Student B

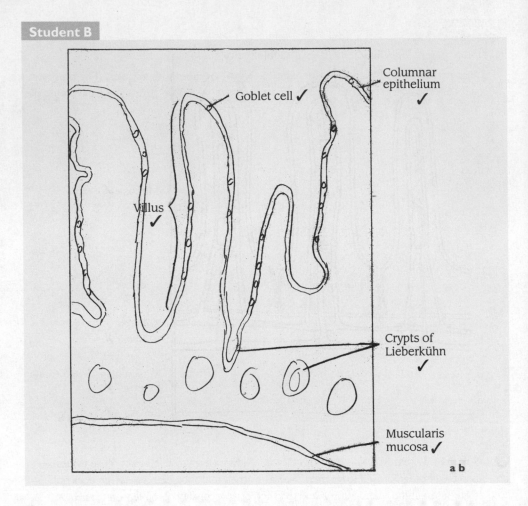

Columnar
epithelium ✓

Goblet cell ✓

Villus ✓

Crypts of
Lieberkühn ✓

Muscularis
mucosa ✓

a b

ⓔ **8/9 marks awarded** **a** This is a block drawing showing tissue layers that illustrate all the obvious features. ✓ It is a fair attempt to draw the photograph ✓ and the proportionality of features is sufficiently accurate ✓. However, the lines tend to be sketchy in places, and circular structures, such as those for the goblet cells, are incomplete. ✗ Student B earns 3 marks out of 4 for drawing skills. **b** Five labels are correctly identified, for 5 marks.

Question 6

(a) Enzymes are globular proteins that catalyse metabolic reactions. The diagram below shows the arrangement of the amino acids in an enzyme to which substrates have attached.

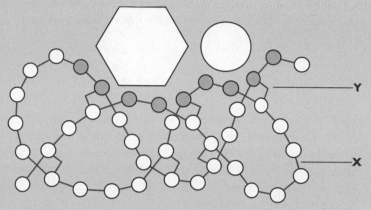

(i) Name the part of the enzyme in which the amino acids are shaded grey. (1 mark)

(ii) Use the diagram and your understanding of enzyme action to explain how an enzyme acts as a catalyst. (3 marks)

(iii) Identify the types of bond labelled **X** and **Y**. (2 marks)

(b) The graph below shows the effect of varying the concentration of sucrose on the activity of the enzyme, sucrase.

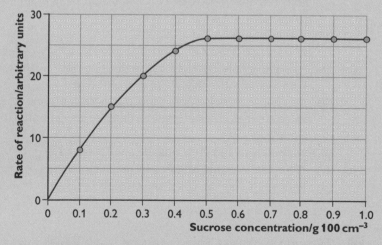

(i) Identify the trends evident in the graph. (2 marks)

(ii) Explain the trends identified. (2 marks)

(iii) Explain how you would control two other variables in this experiment. (2 marks)

(c) The chemical mercaptoethanol breaks (reduces) disulfide links. If the mercaptoethanol is then removed and the enzyme exposed to an oxidising environment, the disulfide links are re-formed.

    (i) Explain the effect that mercaptoethanol would have on the activity of an enzyme.   (1 mark)

    (ii) Explain the effect that heating to temperatures above 45°C would have on the activity of an enzyme such as sucrase? Suggest how this differs from the effect of mercaptoethanol.   (2 marks)

          Total: 15 marks

ⓔ Part (a) relates to enzyme structure and function, and involves mostly recall in (i) and (ii). In (a) (ii), you will benefit from using the diagram to explain how enzymes act as catalysts. In part (b) (i) you must identify trends in a graph of enzyme activity and substrate concentration and then, in (ii), explain the trends. When giving an explanation try to use the word 'because' on the first line of your answer before continuing with a reason. Aspects of experimental design are tested in (b) (iii). Notice that you must do more than just list two variables — you must say how you would control them. In part (c) you need to read the information carefully to determine the effect of the chemical specified.

Student A

(a) **(i)** Active site ✓ **a**

    (ii) They speed up the rate of reaction without being altered themselves. Enzymes bind molecules called substrates and promote the reaction that changes the substrate to products. **b**

    (iii) X — hydrogen bond ✗
           Y — peptide bond ✗ **c**

(b) **(i)** As sucrose concentration increases from 0 to 0.5, the rate of reaction increases. ✓ After this, there is no effect. **d**

    (ii) As more sucrose is added there are more collisions between enzyme and substrate molecules ✓ until the enzyme concentration becomes the limiting factor ✓. **e**

    (iii) Temperature and pH should be controlled. ✗ **f**

(c) **(i)** The enzyme would be killed by mercaptoethanol. ✗ **g**

    (ii) Above 45°C, bonds within the enzyme break and the enzyme becomes inactive. ✓ **h**

ⓔ **5/15 marks awarded a** This is correct, for 1 mark. **b** This answer is not precise enough. It contains nothing about the complementary nature of the active site and substrate or about effectively lowering the activation energy. Student A fails to score. **c** Student A has not looked carefully enough at the diagram: peptide bonds link amino acids into a chain (so bond X); disulfide, ionic or hydrogen bonds link amino acids into folds (so bond Y). Student A fails to score. **d** The first point is correct, for 1 mark. In the second point, 'after this' suggests a time element, which is not present. Furthermore, it is not that there is no effect — the rate of reaction is high. The

CCEA AS Biology

point is that after 0.5 g 100 cm^{-3}, there is *no further increase* in the rate of reaction. **e** This good answer, with correct reference to both trends, scores 2 marks. **f** These are variables that should be controlled, but the question asks *how* they might be controlled. **g** Since enzymes are not themselves alive, they cannot be killed. **h** The effect of heating is explained, but there is no attempt to suggest how the heating effect differs from the effect of mercaptoethanol. Therefore, Student A scores only 1 mark.

Student B

(a) **(i)** Active site ✓ **a**

(ii) The reaction takes place on the active site, which has a complementary shape to that of the substrate molecules. ✓ Enzymes effectively lower the activation energy needed for the reaction ✓ by orientating the substrates in such a way as to facilitate bonding between them ✓. **b**

(iii) X — hydrogen bonds ✗; Y — disulfide bonds ✓ **c**

(b) **(i)** The rate of reaction increases as substrate concentration increases, up to 0.5 g 100 cm^{-3}. ✓ Above this concentration of sucrose, the rate of reaction levels off. ✓ **d**

(ii) As the sucrose concentration is increased, there are more collisions between the enzymes' active sites and the substrate molecules so more enzyme–substrate complexes are formed. ✓ **e**

(iii) A pH buffer should be used to keep pH constant. ✓ Temperature should be controlled using a water bath with the temperature being monitored using a thermometer. ✓ **f**

(c) **(i)** It would temporarily inhibit the enzyme, as it loses its active site, though when mercaptoethanol is removed the enzyme will become active again. ✓ **g**

(ii) At high temperature bonds holding the enzyme in a precise shape are broken and the enzyme is denatured. ✓ This is permanent damage, while the effect of mercaptoethanol is not. ✓ **h**

🄴 **13/15 marks awarded a** This is correct, for 1 mark. **b** This excellent answer gains all 3 marks. **c** X represents a peptide bond, so Student B scores only 1 mark. **d** Both trends are described clearly, for 2 marks. **e** This is correct as far as it goes, for 1 mark. However, Student B has forgotten to explain *why* the graph levels off — at high concentrations of substrate the active sites of the enzyme molecules are saturated. **f** These are complete answers and 2 marks are scored. **g** This is correct, for 1 mark. **h** This correct answer earns 2 marks.

Question 7

(a) The diagram below shows part of a **DNA** molecule in the process of replication.

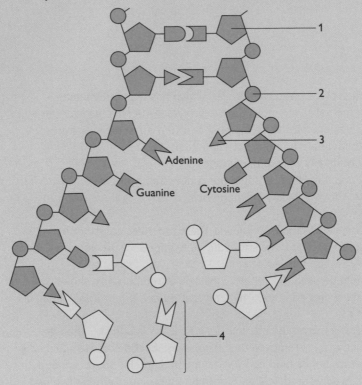

(i)   Name the structures labelled 1 to 4.   (4 marks)
(ii) Name the enzyme which catalyses the attachment of structure 4 to the **DNA** strand.   (1 mark)
(iii) What term is used to describe the mechanism by which **DNA** replicates?   (1 mark)

(b) The **DNA** of each person is different. Differences in the **DNA** may be analysed using restriction endonuclease enzymes that cut **DNA**, producing fragments of different lengths.

(i)   Explain why a specific restriction endonuclease enzyme cuts two **DNA** samples to produce a different number of fragment lengths.   (2 marks)
(ii) What term is used to describe the various lengths of **DNA** from different people as revealed by analysis using endonuclease enzymes?   (1 mark)
(iii) A particular **DNA** fragment may be located using a **DNA** probe. Explain what is meant by **DNA** probe.   (2 marks)

Total: 11 marks

ⓔ Part (a) is straightforward. You should give precise names of the structures in (a) (i). Aspects of DNA replication are tested in (a) (ii) and (iii). In part (b) (i) and (ii) you have to show your understanding of the role of restriction endonuclease enzymes in fragmenting DNA samples and, in (iii), explain the role of a DNA probe.

Student A

(a) **(i)** 1 — pentose sugar ✗
2 — phosphate ✓
3 — organic base ✗
4 — ATP ✗ **a**
(ii) DNA polymerase ✓ **b**
(iii) The S phase ✗ **c**
(b) **(i)** This enzyme cuts the DNA at sites that have a specific base sequence. ✓ **d**
(ii) Restriction fragment length polymorphism ✓ **e**
(iii) A probe is a short length of single-stranded DNA ✓ **f**

ⓔ **5/11 marks awarded a** Structure 1 is deoxyribose; pentose is not precise enough to gain the mark. Structure 3 is an organic base, but should be identified as thymine (will pair with adenine opposite). Structure 4 has an adenine, a deoxyribose but only one phosphate so cannot be ATP. Student A earns 1 mark for naming structure 2 correctly. **b** This is correct, for 1 mark. **c** The S phase is the stage in the cell cycle during which DNA replication takes place. The mechanism is known as semi-conservative replication. Student A fails to score. **d** Student A understands the recognition sites of endonuclease enzymes. However, as there is no mention of why a different number of fragment lengths are produced, Student A earns only 1 mark. **e** This is correct, for 1 mark. **f** The answer is incomplete since no mention has been made of either the probe or the target DNA containing a known nucleotide (base) sequence. This answer would not distinguish a DNA probe from a primer (used in the PCR). 1 mark only scored.

Student B

(a) **(i)** 1 — pentose (5C) sugar ✗
2 —phosphate ✓
3 — nitrogen-containing base ✗
4 — nucleotide ✓ **a**
(ii) DNA helicase ✗ **b**
(iii) Semi-conservative replication ✓ **c**
(b) **(i)** The endonuclease enzyme only cuts at a specific base sequence ✓ and the DNA of different individuals possesses a different number of these recognition sites. ✓ **d**
(ii) DNA fingerprinting ✗ **e**
(iii) A short length of single-stranded DNA ✓ with a specific base sequence ✓ that will attach to a specific section of DNA. **f**

ⓔ **7/11 marks awarded a** Deoxyribose is a more accurate answer for structure 1, as is thymine for structure 3. Student B scores 2 marks. **b** DNA helicase is the enzyme that breaks the hydrogen bonds to 'unzip' the two strands of DNA. The answer is DNA polymerase. The student fails to score. **c** This is correct, for 1 mark. **d** This excellent answer earns both marks. **e** DNA profiling or fingerprinting uses a variety of techniques to determine the differences in the DNA of different individuals. The specific answer required here is restriction fragment length polymorphism. No mark can be awarded. **f** This excellent answer earns both marks.

ⓔ **Section A total for Student A: 27 marks out of 60. Section A total for Student B: 51 marks out of 60.**

Unit 1: Molecules and Cells

Section B

Quality of written communication is awarded a maximum of 2 marks in this section.

Question 8

(a) Describe the structure of the cell-surface (plasma) membrane. (7 marks)

(b) Explain how membrane structure determines how molecules pass through the membrane. (6 marks)

Quality of written communication (2 marks)

Total: 15 marks

ⓔ Part (a), on the structure of the cell-surface membrane, is relatively straightforward. You should organise your thoughts by writing a plan of all that needs to be included so that when you come to write your ideas are well sequenced. A plan will be even more important in part (b) if you are not to miss some important aspects of membrane transport. Throughout you need to be careful in your use of time — you really should not spend more than 20 minutes on this question. Remember too that you will want to have some time to go over earlier parts of the paper.

Student A

(a) The cell membrane is composed of proteins ✓ floating in a fluid bilayer of lipid. This structure is called the fluid-mosaic model. ✓ It is made of two layers of phospholipids ✓ that have heads and tails. The tails of these two layers face each other with the heads facing in opposite directions. The tails are non-polar ✓ and the heads are polar ✓. Proteins consist of long chains of amino acids. Some of these are polar and some aren't. Some rest on the surface of the bilayer while others go right through. **a**

(b) Proteins may act as carriers. Other proteins act as enzymes. Cells have to be recognised by antibodies and hormones because of proteins on the surface. Water is able to pass between the phospholipid molecules of the bilayer because they are very small. ✓ Water-soluble substances also use this route. Glucose, which is polar, relies on carrier proteins. ✓ Facilitated diffusion takes substances against the concentration gradient. **b; QWC c**

ⓔ **8/15 marks awarded a** Five appropriate points are given. In some cases, however, the marks are only just arrived at. 'Bilayer of lipid' is not sufficient to earn a mark, though a following sentence describes 'two layers of phospholipids'. Marks are awarded over two sentences for polar heads facing outermost and non-polar tails facing innermost. The comment about some of the amino acids in the proteins being polar and some being non-polar is not sufficient to earn a mark. Student A should have stated that the amino acids in contact with the lipid layer are non-polar. Further, in the last sentence it is not clear whether 'some' refers to proteins or amino acids. **b** Two appropriate points are provided. Some points are simply wrong, e.g. lipid-soluble substances (not water-soluble) pass directly through the bilayer while facilitated diffusion moves substances down (not against) the concentration gradient. Other points are not relevant: proteins acting as enzymes or hormone receptors have nothing to do with movement across the membrane. **c** Student A expresses ideas clearly, though not always fluently, and the account has sometimes strayed from the point. 1 mark is awarded for quality of written communication.

Student B

(a) The cell surface membrane consists of a bilayer of phospholipids. ✓ The heads of phospholipids are polar and hydrophilic, so they are arranged outermost in water. ✓ The tails of the phospholipids are non-polar and hydrophobic, so they remain in contact with each other. ✓ There are proteins ✓ interspersed among the fluid phospholipids, so the structure is described as a fluid-mosaic model ✓. There are intrinsic proteins that are embedded within the bilayer and there are extrinsic proteins. ✓ Some proteins have carbohydrate attached ✓ and this acts as a cell recognition feature. Cholesterol is also present among the phospholipids and stabilises the fluidity of the membrane, ✓ especially when the temperature changes. **a**

(b) Small gaps in the phospholipids allow entry of small, polar molecules such as water, CO_2 and O_2 by simple diffusion. ✓ Molecules that are too large and polar must pass through protein channels. ✓ Each has a site for a specific molecule so there are many different types of protein channel for different types of molecule. ✓ Carrier proteins can also change shape — a molecule binds to the protein, it changes shape and the molecule is released inside the cell. ✓ Facilitated diffusion is passive, ✓ requiring no energy input. Active transport goes against the concentration gradient and requires energy in the form of ATP. ✓ Where active transport takes place, there is a large number of mitochondria. **b; QWC c**

ⓔ 15/15 marks awarded **a** Eight marking points are given, so the student scores all 7 marks. **b** Six appropriate points are provided, for 6 marks. **c** This is a well-structured account with the ideas expressed fluently. The relationship between membrane structure and how substances pass across the membrane is clearly made. 2 marks are awarded for quality of written communication.

ⓔ **Section B total for Student A: 8 marks out of 15. Section B total for Student B: 15 marks out of 15.**

ⓔ **Paper total for Student A: 35 marks out of 75, a sound grade E. Many marks are missed as a result of a lack of thorough revision. Evaluative skills might have been better had greater practice been undertaken in this area.**

Paper total for Student B: 66 marks out of 75, a grade A. The overall impression is of a thorough knowledge of the unit content, with a more than adequate array of skills in the application of that knowledge.

Knowledge check answers

1 Water molecules are charged and so surround ions and other charged molecules, separating them in solution. Molecules that lack a charged group, i.e. non-polar molecules (e.g. lipids), will not dissolve in water.

2 Heat

3 $C_7H_{14}O_7$

4 Starch molecules can differ in the relative amounts of amylose and amylopectin, and in the number of glucose molecules contained in each.

5 Being more highly branched means that glucose can be more rapidly hydrolysed from glycogen. This is important since animals have relatively high rates of respiration (metabolism) and so use up glucose quickly.

6 *Any two from*: amylose is a polymer of α-glucose, cellulose of β-glucose; amylose is helical, cellulose forms a straight chain; β-glucoses are inverted in cellulose, α-glucoses are not inverted in amylose.

7 A triglyceride is not composed of repeating sub-units — it has three fatty acids attached to a glycerol.

8 A triglyceride consists of three fatty acids bonded to a glycerol, while a phospholipid consists of two fatty acids and a phosphate bonded to a glycerol, i.e. one fatty acid is replaced by a phosphate.

9 The primary structure is held by peptide bonds; the secondary structure by hydrogen bonds; and the tertiary by hydrogen, ionic and disulfide bonds.

10 *Similarities*: both have a quaternary structure (consisting of more than one polypeptide); both are found in animals. *Differences*: haemoglobin consists of four polypeptides while collagen has three; two types of polypeptide occur in haemoglobin while in collagen they are identical; haemoglobin is globular (has a tertiary structure) while collagen lacks a tertiary structure and is fibrous; haemoglobin is conjugated (containing haem groups) while collagen is not; haemoglobin has a functional role (carries oxygen) while collagen has a structural role.

11 **(a)** The formation of maltose from starch is catabolic.
   (b) The synthesis of starch is anabolic.

12 The activation energy is the energy barrier that has to be overcome before the reaction can happen.

13 This is because the enzyme's active site has a precise shape and distinctive chemical (bonding) properties so that only a particular type of substrate molecule can bind.

14 **(a)** An increase in substrate concentration increases the rate of reaction since there is a greater chance of collision with an enzyme molecule.
   (b) An increase in enzyme concentration does not increase the rate of reaction since the enzyme is already present in excess.

15 Denaturation breaks bonds (hydrogen and ionic) in the tertiary structure of the enzyme. This alters the shape of the active site and the substrate is unable to bind to the enzyme.

16 Little or no maltose would be produced.

17 Non-competitive (and permanent)

18 *Any three from*: the rate of reaction of the free enzyme is slightly greater between 0°C and 35°C; the optimum temperature of the immobilised enzyme covers a wider range; the immobilised enzyme begins to denature at a higher temperature; the free enzyme is particularly more active at 40°C.

19 Two

20 Phosphate at one end (the 5′ end) and a pentose sugar at the other (the 3′ end).

21 Chains running alongside one another, but in opposite directions.

22 TAGACAT

23 75% light and 25% intermediate

24 Six

25 Microsatellite repeat sequence; it would differ by the number of 'AT's in the sequence.

26 At the start of each cycle of the PCR, the DNA is heated to break the hydrogen bonds (denature the DNA) and separate the two strands. Taq DNA polymerase is able to remain stable during this DNA denaturation step (and so fresh polymerase enzyme does not have to be added during each cycle).

27 Both are short, single-stranded sequences of DNA complementary to the DNA strand to which they will attach. However, primers are used in the PCR to attach to the ends of the DNA strands to allow binding of the DNA polymerase enzyme since it cannot bind directly to single-stranded DNA fragments, while probes are used to detect the presence of a base sequence in a strand of sought-after DNA (the target DNA, possibly a desired gene) and are labelled (e.g. fluorescently) to allow their location to be identified.

28 To increase the quantity of DNA because the sample obtained from a crime scene may be very small.

29 ×1500

30 **(a)** *Any three from*: cellulose cell wall; plasmodesmata; sap vacuole; chloroplasts; starch grains
   (b) Cell wall of chitin; lysosomes; glycogen granules

31 **(a)** Smooth ER
   (b) Mitochondria
   (c) Centrioles

32 **(a)** Golgi body
   (b) Mitochondrion
   (c) Chloroplast

33 **(a)** Protein synthesis
   (b) Secretion
   (c) Absorption

34 **(a)** The nucleolus produces the components of ribosomes.
   (b) Proteins are made on the ribosomes, enter the rough ER and are encased in vesicles which pinch off and fuse with the forming face of the Golgi body where they are modified and again encased in vesicles which pinch off the mature face.

35 A nucleic acid (DNA or RNA) core and a protein coat.

36 *Any three from*: viruses lack any metabolism (e.g. respiration); lack any organelles, which specialise in metabolic activities, or cytoplasm; possess only one type of nucleic acid; cannot themselves reproduce.

37 TATACATGAG

38 They differ in the number and types of proteins they contain; in the types of carbohydrate within the glycocalyx; and whether cholesterol is present (as in animal membranes). They all have a phospholipid bilayer, though the phospholipids may contain different fatty acids.

39 They have the specific receptor for the attachment of insulin.

40 It should be small and lipid soluble (to pass quickly through the phospholipid bilayer).

41 Channel proteins form hydrophilic pores, which are often shaped to allow only one type of ion through. Carrier proteins are shaped so that a specific molecule (e.g. glucose) can fit into a complementary site at the membrane surface. When the specific molecule fits, the protein changes shape to allow the molecule through to the other side.

42 Solute dissolves and water molecules cluster around the solute molecules. This reduces the capacity for water molecules to move freely, so that the solute potential decreases and, in consequence, the water potential decreases.

43 The water potential will increase.

44 Both use carrier proteins; active transport requires ATP and occurs against the concentration gradient.

45 It presents a larger surface so that more carrier proteins can be supported.

46 Endocytosis

47 The S phase of interphase

48 During nuclear division, animal cells possess centrioles (which act as a focus for spindle fibres) while plant cells lack centrioles (so spindle fibres are parallel). In animal cells cytokinesis occurs by cleavage, while in plant cells cytokinesis occurs through cell plate formation.

49 D, d, d (from the left)

50 Haploid, since there is an uneven number of chromosomes which means that they cannot form homologous pairs.

51 (a) 4

(b) 2

52 2 (of the 4)

53 8 (2^3)

54 Epidermis covering the leaf and (columnar) epithelium lining the ileum

55 Because the cell-surface membranes of the epithelial cells are partly composed of proteins (e.g. involved in facilitated diffusion and active transport).

56 Contraction of longitudinal muscle causes pendular movements, while contraction of circular muscle causes local constrictions.

57 Palisade cells lie towards the upper section of the leaf towards the source of light; they are cylindrical, so reducing the number of light-absorbing cell walls; they are packed with chloroplasts, which contain photosynthetic pigments. All of these features maximise light absorption for photosynthesis.

58 Opening during the day facilitates the uptake of CO_2 for photosynthesis, while closing at night reduces the transpirational loss of water.

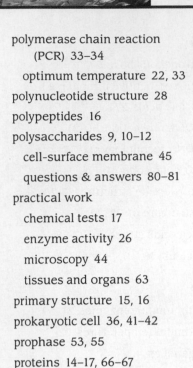